EACH DAY A
NEW HIGH

EACH DAY A NEW HIGH

MARIAN OLIVIA HEATH GRIFFIN

Rev. date: 08/22/2019

To order additional copies of this book, contact:
Xlibris
1-888-795-4274
www.Xlibris.com
Orders@Xlibris.com
801501

CONTENTS

PART THREE

PART ONE

DEDICATED TO:

My parents, Lettie and George Heath, my sisters, Nancy and Hattie E, who taught Mary Drucilla, my niece to have faith in God and herself, her children, Derika & Andrew.

PART TWO

DEDICATED TO:

Leslie's Beloved wife, Roszeta, and children, Leslie III., Wendy & Aria Williams

PART THREE

DEDICATED TO:

Eleanor's family, Nephew -Felton, Helen, Tonya & Nicole Niece, Agnus Davis Patterson and family Husband's children: James C. Miles, Jr., Louella Miles and Tracie Miles Young

AUTHOR'S NOTES

I think I'll run on, see what the end will be. Just before we get ready for New Year or for that proverbial new day, I ponder this biblical verse: "For I am about to do something new."

I am reminded as I begin cleaning my house or cleaning out my closets, I have old things to get rid of. Cleaning my pantry yesterday helped me understand that there are issues to throw away before I can accept exciting new opportunities to grow and serve Christ and others. I have to get rid of some of the debris before new adventures can come into fruition.

Before we make plans for a new day, we would do well to engage in self-evaluation.

"Be strong and courageous. Do not fear or be in dread, for it is the Lord your God who goes with you." (Deuteronomy 31: 6, ESV.)

Next month I will be eighty, no, not eighty months, but eighty years old. I never thought of living eighty years when I was thirty, forty or even fifty. And it didn't just happen. I have been in some serious bumps and issues and at that moment, I could not see my way out.

JESUS! JESUS! My way was cleared for me.

Some people think that "Life doesn't give many second changes. On the other hand, I believe that God gives us second chances each and every day.

I was talking to my first- born niece, Mary Drucilla, some time ago. She was describing the many trials and tribulations she had experienced in her young life as a child.

Lots of children are dealing with adult situations and need help to bounce back into a more secure life. Insecurity is a struggle for everyone, but it is even harder for children.

It is not always easy to get through hurtful times and struggles especially as a child or teenager. Without proper access to enough food and water, a decent and standard living condition, a healthy active lifestyle, children can suffer academically, physically, emotionally and mentally. It is often said, "Children are our future" and it is crucial that they have all they need to succeed.

We should keep in mind that insecurities because of injustice and malpractices on our communities aren't issues that just go away. They are long standing and often need addressing beyond the family.

God is aware of every act of injustice and corruption on earth, and He has promised that soon "the wicked will be cut off from the earth." (Proverbs 2: 22, NIV.)

Moreover, there are many unknowns in life. A personal friend of mine, Leslie Peter, has grappled with health issues for many years in his life. Coupled with earthly disasters, there is still a struggle in his family. He has often needed support of friends and loved ones to secure a place under the sun. Sometimes, he needs an advocate to combat the hurt and pain he has to endure. Experiences don't stop. They grow with you. When life's biggest challenges step into our space, we need the assistance of sustainable action to combat what we cannot do for ourselves.

God answers prayer and we can count on Him to be active throughout the devastations and hardships we encounter. He sends help every time or helps us have the encouragement and strength to pick up the pieces and move on.

A special elderly friend, Eleanor, who was desirous of becoming my daughter, Karen's 'Grandmother Gee Gee', has lived and lived and lived. She is over one hundred and two years old.

She has had many defining moments in her life. She recognizes that we as a human race have more in common than we do than what separates us. She is a strong individual with a great sense of humor, and goes to bat for anyone in need.

She tells me if you don't like something that is going wrong, don't just sit there, do something about it. When it comes to tough issues, we complain but are too afraid to speak up and speak out.

It is impossible to ignore Eleanor. She is one of a kind. She has accomplished much in her lifetime and will tell you about it.

Eleanor is still aware of everything that's going on around her. Why make life harder or busier than it has to be.

Marc and Angel Chernoff, in their book, GETTING BACK TO HAPPY, said. A big reason so many of us fill our lives with needless busyness has to do with the always-plugged in, always connected, always sharing, always comparing society we live in. We default to defining ourselves based on where we are and what we have in relation to everyone else. If we don't have a "better" career, house, car or pair of shoes, we feel inferior. And the only way we can possibly do better is to be busier doing -whatever." (p. 41.)

Someone once said:

> "Peace does not mean to be in a place where there is no noise,
> trouble or hardwork.

These three persons, Mary Drucilla, Leslie Peter and Eleanor have given me permission to deal with their lives in order to help and show someone else that God never sleeps. He is always there to help His children in season and out of season.

God helps us deal with the realities of living in a fallen world with its disappointing relationships, unfulfilled longings and shattered dreams. God meets you wherever you are in the midst of your turmoil and sufferings and enables you to see a new day from His perspective.

As a result, even in the face of heartache and tears, they could praise their God with joy because of a deeper intimacy with God.

> They all have been given new chances in life
> There is such a thing as Spiritual healing.
> Jesus has a vision for us, the ones He created.

He longs to unearth the beauty in us that He created in us.

"He can change your reality and thoughts and turn your trials into triumphs." (Chernoff, p. 41.)

"Sometimes it is painful. Other times it is uncomfortable. But God has promised to work with us and through us until the day when His glory and beauty are fully revealed in our lives." (Susanna Foth Aughtmon.)

Lyanla Vanzant, in her book, LIVING THROUGH THE MEANTIME, relates this message:

"Spiritual healing requires a willingness to forgive, the courage to release fear and the readiness to relinquish anger, guilt and shame. It is in those acts that we develop the ability to see God in everyone, including ourselves." (p. 11.)

I tell my children and grandchildren, "Every life has a mission. It is often difficult to actualize that mission. Mainly because we don't know what our mission is.

M. Scott Peck said in his book, FURTHER ALONG THE ROAD LESS TRAVELED, "no one knows. We dwell in a profoundly mysterious universe. In the words of Thomas Edison, "We don't even begin to understand one percent about ninety-nine percent of anything." (p. 67.)

I tell my folk, "But God knows. He makes the impossible, possible. Every day is different. If you have trouble verbalizing your feelings and longings, God will help you put into words what's in your heart."

I find it a joy to be near these three individuals because I always get a big laugh, a big hug and a quick up- lift. They quickly improve my mood even when we are discussing problems and solutions.

No wonder the Scripture says, "A cheerful heart is good medicine."

I realize that I feel closer to God and Christ when I can laugh and see the beauty and humor in whatever circumstances exist.

Jeanette Hanscome said in MORNINGS WITH JESUS, Vol. 5, No. 1, "Seeing Jesus' sense of fun reflected in creation reminds me that He is the ultimate source of joy and that we serve a Lord who understands that with all that life throws at us, sometimes the best thing we can do is laugh."

With prayer and praise and worship of God, we can experience God in a fresh deeper way. We have seen change and hope with illness and heartache because of prayer.

FAST FORWARD- ANOTHER SHOOTING, NO TWO

Lord, when will we have "Each Day a new high!"
This is the here and now!
"August 3, 2019 is my husband, Bertrand Griffin's birthday and Barack Obama's birthday is on August 4, 2019. Both of these days were supposed to be a new High."

"Didn't I tell you that God made His creation and He made only ONE BLOOD. He is the giver of every good and perfect gift. We as a people do not have to scramble and pierce each other for God's love and grace."

"Hope deferred makes the heart sick," says Proverbs13:12, NIV.

"Believing that God will do what He said is quite different from waiting for Him to do it. We mess our lives with do-it- yourself projects when God has promised the best for each of us."

We are all connected. God has provided for all of us. We should feel a togetherness in God's universe. Yet, we are more apart than ever. I am so frustrated and sad. The song writer, Isaac Watts said:

> O GOD, OUR HELP IN AGES PAST.
> OUR HOPE FOR YEARS TO COME,
> OUR SHELTER FROM THE STORMY BLAST,
> AND OUR ETERNAL HOME.
>
> WORDS: Isaac Watts, 1719 (Ps. 90.)
> THE UNITED METHODIST HYMNAL.

The psalmist said:

> For a thousand years in your sight,
> Are like a day gone by,
> Or like a watch in the night.
> You sweep me away in the sleep of the night.
> They are like the new grass in the morning.
> Though in the morning it springs up new.
>
> (Psalms 90: 4-6, NIV.)

ACKNOWLEDGEMENTS

LET ME ACKNOWLEDGE MY GOD for my diverse ancestors and my parents, Lettie Harper Heath and George Wesley Heath. Were it not for them, we would not exist. God made one blood for which I thank Him. My mother taught my siblings and me, Phyllis (deceased), George W, Jr, Daniel (deceased) Joseph, Nancy and Hattie E (deceased) that we were too mixed up to hate anyone.

These are the persons who were in my household when I was growing up. These persons were the deciding factors that molded my young life. With them, I learned so much, especially from my parents and grandparents who helped me through sharing experiences and encouraging me to choose hope and faith instead of fear and dismay.

I am thankful to be the parents of Bertrand, II (Kotosha), Karen (Keith Phenix), and Michael, Tracie.) They have always been my pride and joy even when they were young and required so much attention and care. As adults, they are resourceful in my research for authentic and documentary materials. They are all my talking buddies.

I owe a special thanks to Bertrand, II and Keith for editing my first book. I am grateful to them both. Keith, our son-in-law has edited other books for me for which I am so thankful.

Then my eight grandchildren, Nia Olivia, Kiara Janelle, Christian-Paris, Amelia -Grai, Victoria Olivia, Olivia Christina and Sophia Morgan, my grand-god children, Amelia and Warren Pleasant, and my great niece, Amoree Sanders are very precious to me.

I acknowledge my St. Mark clergy: Rev. Simon Chigumira, Senior pastor, Rev. Bertrand Griffin, Rev. Glorious Wright and Rev Willie Laws (all retired.)

My St. Mark United Methodist Church family is very special to me, especially the Cherubim Choir, past and present (which I established forty-seven years ago and still play for). The Sanctuary Choir and Female Ensemble are choirs that I sing in.

I acknowledge other members of our church including Lorita Frank, Charlotte Burkhalter, Vinnie Davis, Dorothy Collins, Rozalyn Magee, Michelle Thomas, Eunice Simmons, Sophia Ennin, Edwina Jackson, Terrie Sanderford, Catherine and Semmie Martin, Edna Hickman and her sister, Lottie Brown and others.

We formed a NINETY-PLUS group when Eleanor Miles said she was making her ninety first birthday and asked me to take her picture. We established the Ninety-Plus group because Eleanor said there was no one to look out for elderly people in our church.

That day I took pictures of Eleanor S. Miles, Mildred Bowie, Doris Thompson Eloise Williamson, Mable Jackson, Mary Taylor, Nathalie Holloman, Alice Stepter and Vertlee Washington (who moved from New Orleans after the Katrina Hurricane and flood in 2005.)

We started a special birthday party celebration each year for this group and have added others: Emily Marshall, Ruth Myers, Ruth Eby, Ella Pitts, Mary Matthews and Milton Grayer. Eleanor and four others are over one hundred years old. Some have passed on. St. Mark church has changed administrations and pastors but the Ninety-Plus group still stands.

I am grateful for the genealogy staff at the East Baton Rouge Main library on Goodwood Boulevard for all the assistance in doing my research.

Thanks to the library staff at the Scotlandville branch who have been so helpful. They include: Pamela A Donaldson, Jennifer I Thompson, Chad Cooper and Charles Shropshire.

I am honored to acknowledge many special friends who have been supportive of me over the years: Dr. Leslie and Roszeta Norris, Dr. Jonathan and Geraldine Roberts, Dr. Jesse L Douglas, Dr. Robert and Helen Williams(decease) and Dr. George and May Calvin Belton (deceased.)

Let me thank the members of my Alpha Kappa Alpha sorority for their support: including Karen Griffin- Phenix (daughter), Sanettria Glasper Pleasant, Janifer B. Peters, Lorita Frank, Sandra T. Hall, Gloria and Carmen Spooner, Judy P. Reed, Dr. Katina Semien, Esq. (South Central Regional Director), Dr. Lovenia Deconge-Watson, Geraldine and Joni Roberts, Marilyn Ray-Jones, Susie Boudreaux, Gwen and Jaimelle Thomas, Kismet Gray, Doveal Essix, Marvis H. Lewis, Myrtle Joyner, Melba Moye, Tamara Montgomery and Dr. Julia B. Purnell – Sixteenth International President(deceased), and so many others.

Gamma Eta Omega chapter of ALPHA KAPPA ALPA SORORITY continues to make a viable presence in the lives of so many people and the world.

I am honored to be in the family of so many great people: Sally Gillespie Newman, Brenda and Diane Cooks, Edwin Cooks and Linda Cooks Narcisse, (Johnnie), Janet Nock Moreno, Martin Anthony Nock, Sandra Brickhouse, Rose Kelly, and Bessie Lawrence and family.

I recently became re -acquainted with friends and relatives I had not seen for many years: Medford "Lee Lee" Freshwater, his children, Trinka and Dr. Mullin, Michael, Lucille Freshwater Harmon and her husband, James Harmon, Rev. Gayle H., Rev. Braven O. Duffie, Eleanor L. Fooks, Robert Chandler and a host of others.

Special thanks to my little cousin, Janet Nock Moreno, for her embracing me and reminding me through research and documents of who we are as a family, as a people. She dared me to write a book about our family:

"Good Luck, Marian. That's a hard job. You are setting yourself up for much work!"

"I have written nine books since that conversation."

To: "Elaine Sims and the Beauty Shop bunch, you are so inspiring."

Throughout my life time, there have been many exchanges with other people- experiences shares and struggles endured. I have been into contact with some beautiful human beings. Many names of relatives, friends and co-workers such as Mary Bradford Veronica Carter, Lois Waterson and Safronia Amos have made an impact on my life. In another capacities, my co-workers at Southern University inspired me: Rose Roche and Terrell Jackson.

I have much to be thankful for which never ceases to amaze me.

My story belongs to me but so many people have entered my life and inspired me as I travel on this journey. Many persons have helped me take out whatever is stressing me and get rid of it. They may not have ever been aware of what they did for me. I acknowledge you though I may not know your name.

The first shall be last and the last shall be first. I always save the acknowledgement of my husband, Bertrand, Sr. because I always have so much to say to him and about him. I am so proud of his accomplishments.

When I met him and married him, he was attending Gammon Theological Seminary (Interdenominational Theological Seminary), where he received his Bachelor's and Master's degrees in Sacred Theology.

He attended Purdue University in West Lafayette, Indiana for special training by the Board of Global Ministries to work with the Migrant Ministry, he attended Northwestern University in Evanston, Illinois for special training in working in the United Methodist Church.

He received a grant for special training in Crisis Counseling and Endorsement for working as a Chaplain in Prison Ministry. He received his training for Crisis Counseling at the New Orleans Baptist Theological Seminary at the New Orleans Baptist Hospital and his Endorsement from a Methodist Institute in Washington, D.C.

Bertrand, Sr. has helped so many people to be rehabilitated out of the prison system of Louisiana as chaplain. He was chaplain at Louisiana State Penitentiary for four years and Senior Chaplain at Dixon Correctional Institute for over thirty years. Some of these rehabilitated prisoners have become ministers.

Bertrand, Sr still works with prisoners who have left the penal system. He has served as pastor of two United Methodist churches before receiving the special call in chaplaincy ministry. A retired United Methodist minister and chaplain, Bertrand, Sr still serves on committees and gives service to his local church.

Let me just say thanks to God for my husband who came into my life at such a strategic time. God wants us to turn to him for help with our most intimate concerns. Then Jehovah, in His unselfish love, promises to provide "the peace of God that surpasses all understanding." (Philippians 4:6-7, NIV.)

I LOVE AND APPRECIATE ALL OF YOU IN MY LIFE!

INTRODUCTION

HISTORICAL PERSPECTIVE

Some persons are born at risk. It may be because some individuals make bad decisions or take wrong turns. Seeking God's help first before you turn to physical assistance often leads to unexpected answers or directions. Pray first, then wait. We should never underestimate the importance of our prayers for ourselves and others. Oftentimes, someone else's ministry helps us weather the storms of life.

God displays power, justice and wisdom. The Bible does not say that God is power. It says that He is love. Why? Because it says that God's power enables Him to act and His justice and wisdom guide the way for us. Love, moreover, influences everything He does.

The early church understood the power and connection between our prayers and sending out Missionaries to share the good news to others. The first believers were "worshiping the Lord and fasting" when the "Holy Spirit instructed them to set apart for me Barnabas and Saul (Paul) for the work to which I have called them. Then they "fasted and prayed and "placed their hands on them" and prayed again and "sent them off." (Acts 13: 2-3, NIV.)

At the beginning of his letter to the church in Ephesus, Paul tells the believers how he had been praying for them:

"I pray that the eyes of your heart may be enlightened in order that you may know the hope to which He has called you, the riches of His glorious inheritance in His holy people." (Ephesians 1:18, NIV.)

"The heart, from a biblical perspective, is the center of our being, instrumental in all of our decisions and actions. God's word tells us that "the human heart is the most deceitful of all things, and desperately wicked" (Jeremiah 17:9, NIV.)

Yet, His unselfish love moved him to create intelligent human beings both earthly and heavenly, who benefit from and enjoy His love and care. And He continually shows love to all humans in that "He makes his sun to rise on both the wicked and the good. He makes it rain on both the righteous and the unrighteous." (Matthew 5:45, NIV.)

Jesus said that "it is from within, out of a person's heart, that evil thoughts come – sexual immorality, theft, murder, adultery, greed, malice, deceit, envy, slander and folly." (Mark 7:21-22.)

Oftentimes some individual's decisions affect others to the extent that whole generations are impacted. The Lord can remove any obstacle and free them from their chains.

"We pray for God to open the eyes of those we are trying to reach with His love, asking that their hearts will be flooded with light." (Ephesians 1:18, NIV.)

TODAY IS A NEW DAY, BUT NOT HIGH!

I did not know I was going to have to write this 'chapter' from a historical perspective. It will forever be written in the time of men, but especially for me. Today is my husband Bertrand Griffin's eighty-fifth birthday, August 3, 2019.

One day later and we have our forty-fourth President, Barack Obama's birthday on August 4, 2019. These are two of the greatest men that ever lived and are still living (in my opinion.)

Yet, these two days, in a thirteen -hour time period are the hosts of two of the greatest tragedies known to man. A young white man, his whole life ahead of him, drove ten hours from Dallas, Texas to El Paso, Texas to shoot as many Mexicans and other Hispanic people as he could.

"Did he stop to get gas; did he stop at McDonald's or the Subway to get a sandwich? I wonder.

"I wonder if he did all the normal things that a traveler would do, or did he risk running out of gas and being hungry to get to his destination and carry out this evil deed."

Since the beginning of time brothers were killing brothers, sisters were doing evil things to each other. Nations were fighting nations. Groups of people divided themselves into races and sub-races due to the concept of hate.

One shooting in El Paso, Texas left twenty (22) people dead and twenty - four people injured Saturday morning in Wal-Mart store that was located on the border between El Paso and a Mexican town.

Perhaps, most people in that large Wal-Mart store were just buying purchases for their children to start school within the next two weeks. Or they may have been enjoying an outing during the first week in August.

The shooter (Murderer) let us know through media that, he a white man, a 'white supremist', 21 years old was targeting Mexicans who lived within a mile of where they were shot.

This white man admitted that he is frightened that more Hispanics will vote in our next national election than white men. He tried to kill as many as he could.

This news was all over the TV channels by Saturday afternoon.

Daniel, a young eleven- year -old boy, came home from baseball practice, dried tears on his face. He questioned his father.

"Dad, you're a preacher. You are supposed to explained these things. How can one man set out to kill so many people.? Why are things so bad?"

Seeing how frustrated and sad Daniel was, his father set Daniel down.

"Yes, there are evil people in this world. But there are so many good people in this world, also.

A few hours later, preparing to attend church on Sunday morning, August 4, 2019, Daniel's family heard that the next shooting in Dayton Ohio was announced on television.

It had happened within thirteen hours of the shooting in El Paso in Dayton, Ohio. Nine more people were shot dead and twenty more injured, thirteen hundred miles from the El Paso shooting.

Another white man, twenty-four years old shot and killed nine more people and wounded twenty more. How could this be. "How can we go to church as if nothing happened.?"

An accounting of the Ohio shooting was that at least four black women and two black men were killed. The rest of the people were white including the sister of the white, 24 years old shooter. The news reporters did not give the names of these shooters but once. And rightly so. They should not become famous on such despicable crimes. Many times, the Bible did not name the perpetrators of crimes unless they were kings. Our king, 'our president' has been named as one who is leading the white supremacy, the white hate crime movement.

WE ARE IN A HUMANITARIAN CRISIS. So many things are happening as I write and as we recently celebrated World Refugee Day. We had a double drowning of a refugee father and his daughter fleeing persecution and torture from their country. They died in the Rio Grande River fleeing the danger of their homeland."

"This shows one of the darker sides of immigration," said Richard Meek, editor of (THE CATHOLIC COMMENTATOR, August 2, 2019, vol. 57, No. 13. P. 1.)

"The grim reality is perhaps there are millions of immigrants already in our country and to ignore them or send them back to face what is likely certain death in their native country, is akin to turning our backs on the Gospel message. Those persons sitting in border stations, families seeking a new life, are the very people Jesus would have embraced and held in His arms over 2000 years ago."

"These are the same people that Jesus is asking us today to treat with the Christian dignity they deserve."

"It also cannot be overstated that the Holy Family was once a refugee family. We may see this immigration problem play out for many years to come. Bur collectively, as a nation, with political beliefs and prejudices (And racial hatred) shelved, we must ask the question, WHAT WOULD JESUS DO?"

Daniel went to church that morning, hungry for a word that would explain the mystery of prejudice and hurt to other people. Daniel's father, the preacher, couldn't give his child and his congregation a satisfactory answer.

"Why does the Almighty God not set times for judgment? Why must those who know him look in vain for such days?" (Job 24:1, NIV).

"The groans of the dying rise from the city, and the souls of the wounded cry out for help. But God charges no one with wrongdoing." (Job: 1, 12).

Job, in the above passages of Scripture, seeks an answer from God with an emotional question.

This is America! Our Country! Our Creator gave us all one blood. He gave us the wisdom and power to change all of this.

"As heat and drought snatch away the melted snow, so the grave snatches away those who have sinned. The womb forgets them, the worm feasts on them; the wicked are no longer remembered but are broken like a tree." (v.v. 19-20).

They prey on the barren and childless woman and to the widow, they show no kindness (or mercy. (v.v. 19-20).

But God drags away the mighty by his power; though they become established, they have no assurance of life. He may let them rest in a feeling of security, but His eyes are on their ways. For a little while, they are exalted, and then they are gone; they are brought low and gathered up like all others; they are cut off like heads of grain. If this is not so, who can prove me wrong and reduce my words to nothing?" (Job 1: 21-25).

The Scripture writer said, THE BATTLE IS NOT YOURS, IT'S THE LORDS! (II Chronicles 15: 1, NIV.)

O GOD IN HEAVEN
GRANT TO THY CHILDREN,
MERCY AND BLESSING,
SONGS NEVER CEASING

(Elena G. Maquiso, 1961,
THE UNITED METHODIST HYMNAL

WE HAVE OUR BIBLE AS OUR QUIDE, OUR HANDBOOK! (Meek, p. 9.)

PART ONE

CHAPTER I

Mary Drucilla's Struggling Childhood

Mary Drucilla is my first -born niece. She is my oldest sister's child. Mary was born in a small rural town in Accomack County, Virginia on February 8, 1956. Our Grandmother Hattie Wise Heath was a mid-wife in this area and had delivered hundreds of babies including her grandchildren and great grandchildren.

So, it was not an unusual occurrence that she should deliver Mary. Mary was her first great grandchild. Mary's middle name is Drucilla, which is her Great Grandmother Hattie's middle name.

Our grandmother Hattie agreed to keep Baby Mary in her home until Phyllis established herself. Mary Drucilla lived with Grandmom Hattie for eight months. She remembers sleeping in the bed with her great grandmother.

Life has many challenges and people often wonder why or what controls the final outcome.

No less, children wonder where they can find answers to some of the bigger questions that affect their lives.

Mary remembered many things that happened during her childhood, some were pleasant, others were frightening and very hurtful. Many times, she felt rejected by her mother.

Phyllis, Mary Drucilla's mother, brought her from Virginia and moved in with her parents and stayed in Delaware until she had her second child, Billy. Then she and her family, her husband and two children, moved to Philadelphia from our house in Delaware and lived with our Aunt Mary and Uncle Alma Paulson for a while.

Phyllis and Willie, her husband, were able to get temporary jobs but there was no one there to take care of the two small children. Since Phyllis had a job in an industrial plant, Willie's job did not pay as much, so he quit his job to take care of Mary and Billy.

Mary Drucilla said her mother, Phyllis, dressed her beautifully in colorful outfits. One day she put a little pink snowsuit on Mary and took her out in the snow. Mary was put down in white stuff, later identified as snow. Mary didn't want to be put down in the snow. She wanted to stay in her mother's arms. It seemed that her mother was always putting Mary down, first in the snow, then in the wagon, then handing her to someone else. It also seemed that her mother preferred Billy, her new baby brother to her.

Willie left the family and went back to Florida to his own home for a few weeks. He returned to Philadelphia. He brought a large beef tongue with him which didn't look edible. He made the children eat some of the beef tongue which was gross. Billy could not eat the cut-up meat because he was too young.

Billy, Phyllis' second child born on May 30,1857 at the Heath home in Delaware, was receiving much more attention than Mary.

Mary Drucilla began to realize that Willie, her step-father, was getting meaner and more atrocious. That's when he started sexually abusing her. Phyllis began letting Mary sleep with her. It was very cold in the house in Philadelphia. Willie left again, but he came back.

Phyllis had an old car. She packed up and left Philadelphia and returned to Delaware. Willie came along. After all, he couldn't stay in Philadelphia with Phyllis' people, her Aunt Mary and Uncle Alma.

Looking for work again, Phyllis and Willie left Mary and Billy with our parents, Grandmother Lettie and Grandpop George. At first, Mary felt rejected again by her mother.

Guy Winch wrote in his book, EMOTIONAL FIRST AID, "One of the reasons our self-esteem is so vulnerable to rejection is that we are wired with a fundamental need to feel accepted by others. When our need to belong remains unsatisfactory for extended periods of time, either because of the rejections we've experienced or because we lack the opportunities to create supportive relationships, it can have a powerful and detrimental effect on our physical and psychological health." (p. 13.)

When Phyllis and Willie left their children in Delaware this time, the Mary Drucilla started going to elementary school. The children were happy.

They had two aunts, Nancy and Hattie E, to play with and take good care of them.

Mary Drucilla said, "My aunts, Nancy and Hattie E were my idols. They were in high school and I was in elementary school. I started school at five years old. Billie was almost four years old and stayed home with Grandmom Lettie.

All was grand on the home front until Phyllis and Willie came back and got Mary and Billie again and took them to Florida to Willie's family home. That's when the abuse started again with Mary and her step-father.

Many persons in the Bible, including Job, declares "God can do all things; and no plan of yours can be thwarted." (Job 42:2-3, NIV.)

"God will ultimately prevail over all obstacles, restoring the fortunes and good life of those who are faithful. The people of God may pray that He will keep His promise and be gracious to them as He preserves their lives in time of great difficulty." (para. Job 42: 3-4, NIV.)

Phyllis, Mary's mother, returned to Virginia with her husband, Willie Pepper. Phyllis was pregnant again, but she lost that child. She had planned to stay with her grandmother Hattie until her third child was born. When she lost that child, she moved her family to Delaware once more to live with our family, my mother Lettie and father, George Heath.

My sister, Phyllis's family was nomadic. I was in college and was not aware of all of this movement of Phyllis' family.

When I talked to Mary Drucilla about her childhood, she said "I had only spasmatic periods of happiness as a child."

The first year of my life was a happy one. I remember living with Grandmom Hattie for a while in Virginia. (Of course, I did not know where I was, I just knew how my grandmother and others made me feel. Grandmom Hattie held me a lot. She had a store and had many customers. They petted me right along with my grandmother.

Grandmom Hattie would sit me up in a big box with pillows around me while she waited on her customers. Then she would pick me up again and hold me.

"Grandmom Hattie said I laughed a lot. I was happy."

"Then Mom and my step- dad, Willie came and got me from Great Grandmom Hattie's house. We moved into the house with Grandmother Lettie and Grandpop George in Greenwood, Delaware. I had two aunts, Nancy and Hattie E who once again looked after us and played with us and fed us. Phyllis and Willie, my parents left me there until I was six years old. I learned to crawl, walk, talk and eat solid food at Grandmother Lettie's house. I was well cared for at that house.

Mary told me "Then when we left there, my mother had me and my younger brother, Billy. He had been born at Grandmother Lettie's house. We moved to Florida to Daddy Willie's parent's home.

I was not quite seven years old and Billy was five and a half. I wanted to go back to Greenwood with Grandmom Lettie. She was kind and thoughtful and I had nice people around me and my brother in Greenwood.

"I was sexually abused from the age two and a half to the age of twelve by my step- father, Willie."

Mary Drucilla said, "At first I thought he was just playing with me, because he was openly tickling me on my legs and around my chest area." I think Mom let it happen, because she thought Willie was playing with me, too.

"Then the 'playing got rougher and rougher. I began to be so frightened of Daddy Willie. He started coming into our bedroom (Billy and I slept in the same bedroom), and picking me up and carrying me into the bathroom and touching me all over my body, apparently prepping me for further 'horse play'. That's what he called it.

"I became frightened every time he came into my bedroom. He'd say, "Hush, we're going to do a little "Horse Play." When I'd hear the floor creek, I would know it was him coming after me."

I would hide under the bed or in the closet. If he didn't see me, he would go back out. There were sometimes in the night when he would come several times looking for me. If I fell into a deep sleep, he would grab me and carry me into the bathroom for his "mid-night snack".

"When I tried to call out to Mom, he would say, "Don't bother her, she's asleep or she's sick. There were other people in the house, also. But they didn't seem to care about me."

I found out later that Mom was afraid of him too. She told me after I was grown that she knew he was doing something to me.

"That's why I moved so much, trying to get away from him," Mom said.

"When we went to Florida to stay with his family, His mother would make us move. They didn't want him at their house. And they certainly didn't want us there. It was too many of us to feed."

It was too many of us. So, when I left, Willie would hop back in my car and say, "I'll help you drive. Wherever I stayed, he'd come too. I was his "meal ticket."

"I was fortunate that I had loving relatives, because they never turned us out, even with Willie there," Phyllis, my mom told me.

Mary later told me, "He was very abusive to us, including spanking his son, Billy. But mostly he just wanted to sit and hold Billy until he got a chance to get at me. My life was not easy as a child.

Phyllis and Willie brought Mary and Billy back to Grandmother Lettie's house in Greenwood.

Mary and Billy were happy when they were in the Heath home in Delaware. Mary and Billy went to elementary school in Greenwood, Delaware for several years.

Then Phyllis took them back to Florida with her husband, Willie's home. There was no change there. The verbal and sexual abuse started again. This was the cycle in Mary's life that was so conflicted in her childhood. She just remembers that there were so many times when she was uprooted and taken from one relative's home to another.

Mary's life was at once harsh, bleak and lifeless as a result of Daddy Willie's being a child molester and Mom's inactivity to do anything about it because of her fear of the step-father.

On the other hand, the effect that this had on Mary was to be docile and submissive as well as resigned to her way of life.

Winch said, "Some of us have such challenging life circumstances that satisfying our need (for love) and to belong can present a real challenge. Some face far greater hurtles than most in this regard."

"Once we have suffered profound and repeated pain and rejection over our lifetime, finding our place in the world and feeling as though we belong can be the hardest struggle of all." (p. 13.)

Mary said, "The one thing that I don't remember is when we moved because it was mostly at night. We would just be hauled into my mother's car and travel all night until we reached the next station where we would stay for a while."

Phyllis would get jobs and work in factories and took other jobs when available. Willie was not inclined to work at any job.

"He may get a job working in an auto shop or in a factory but would not keep it long," Mary told me.

Phyllis was trying to keep her family together. She cried many tears, yet her struggles continued. She was so vulnerable and gullible in her relationships.

She and her husband went back to Florida and left her children in Greenwood with Grandmother Lettie and Granddaddy many times. She knew that her children's health and well-being was at stake but was helpless to attend to their needs herself. My two younger teenage sisters were at home which gave Mary and Billy relief. Nancy and Hattie E, as teenagers, helped to care for their niece and nephew. Our mother was sickly and was unable to do much around the house.

The family learned later that Phyllis and Willie had separated and Phyllis had a lawyer send Willie divorce papers. He never signed them. Willie died by drowning in a hotel swimming pool. They found his wallet at the edge of the swimming pool which identified him.

Later in life, Phyllis realized her many weaknesses and confessed to God and her three sisters, Marian, Nancy and Hattie E. She confessed to God and man. She died on August 3, 1997. Phyllis was saved on her death-bed with Hattie E as one of the nurses in the hospital by her side.

CHAPTER II

Mary Drucilla's Conflicted Teenage Years

While Phyllis was away working, she would send money home to Daddy for Mary and Billy's up keep.

Mary said, "By this time, my Grandmother Lettie had died and Esther had moved into our home with Grandpop, George. Then they got married and Esther took over the running of the house. She just wanted us to work around the house all the time. She kept us busy."

"I don't think she wanted us to attend Junior high and high school. I had finished Junior High school and was ready to go to high school. I was about fourteen and ready to go to high school. That would once again be my escape."

"I was getting taller and bigger. I did not have decent clothes to wear to high school," Mary said.

"I had outgrown my childhood clothes. I realized that my clothes were straight out of the frumpville collection. I had only one decent outfit and it was too formal to wear to school every day."

"The other clothes in my closet had permanent spots on them and were also way up my hip," she said.

"I felt excited about catching the bus to Woodbridge and going to high school but also jumbled and challenged. Would I fit in? Will the other teens make fun of me? The clothes in my grandmother's closet were way too small and old fashion; my Aunt Nancy and Hattie E had taken their clothes to college with them."

"I didn't quite know what to do. I started praying. "Lord, what am I going to do?"

"I went to Goodwill Industries and found a house robe that fitted me. I hemmed it up and sewed it up in the middle and put a belt around it. I caught the bus to go to high school. I did that for more than a week. It was getting cold so I could wear a coat."

"I was so ashamed because I heard someone say "That looks like a house dress or a robe.""

"Word got around that I was not dressing properly for high school. One of the neighbors brought me a pair of boots and some clothes to wear. I was not only not getting enough to eat at home, I didn't really have decent teenage clothes to wear."

"This conversation with Mary made me realize just how important having new clothes to start back to school was. Mother Lettie had always bought us new shoes and socks and a new skirt or pants to start back to school in."

I told Mary, "I was always upset and mad because I started back to school around my birthday and I got the same thing that my siblings got, nothing extra."

"How petty was I when I discerned later that my parents were doing the best they could for all of us," I told Mary.

"Mom (Phyllis) told me later that she had been sending money to Grandpop George. He could have bought me some new clothes to wear. Grandpop was giving the money to Esther."

"One day, I slipped up and called my step- grandmother, Esther," said Mary.

Grandpop came home that night and Esther told him that I should have more respect for her. I should not call her 'Esther', I should call her Grandmom Esther.

Grandpop George chastised me severely and told me he would whip me if I called her Esther again.

This vicious cycle that Mary and Billy went through as children unveils the strength that Mary had and the weakness that Billy had. Billy couldn't figure things out. Mary was constantly helping herself by escaping the evils that happened in her life. Over the years, one problem after another had been solved in unexpected ways by the grace of God.

Mary was an avid reader. She was smart, even brilliant like her mother, Phyllis. One major difference between mother and daughter was, Phyllis was smart-mouthed and Mary was humble.

She loved to read. In Junior high and high school, Mary started back to school in Greenwood Junior High and Bridgeville High School. She went to the libraries almost every day to get books.

She read all the classics she could find in the libraries. She read novels. She read non-fiction. She also had a very sharp memory.

Mary remembers the hundreds of book titles and authors today.

Those dreary frustrating years when she was a young teenager, Mary would go upstairs with her books and read into the night and study. Granddaddy George started scolding her for reading so much. Esther had begun lying to Granddaddy about Billy and Mary. Granddaddy George started telling Mary to turn the light out in her room.

Mary found a small lamp and a light bulb around the house. She put it under her bed and would continue reading all night. She would get up early, fix herself and granddaddy some breakfast, (Queen Esther did not get up early and did not want Mary to fix her breakfast.)

I told Mary one time, "My Daddy was not like that with his children. He wanted us to study and read. He even helped me with my math when I was in high school. Why would he act like that with his grandchildren?"

Mary said, "Grandmother Lettie raised all of her children with Granddaddy George. It was a totally different life style. Grandmother Lettie was kind and gentle and Granddaddy George was fun to be with. He played with us and took us to the movie sometimes. We went to church, went to church activities, picnics, the beach and concerts. The feeling of goodness lasted until we went back with Mom and my step-daddy, Willie.

"Mom didn't know Grandmother Lettie had died. She brought us back to live with my grandparents, and found out that Grandmother Lettie had died and was buried uptown in the Greenwood cemetery. She went uptown and sat at the foot of my grandmother's grave, pulling weeds from around the small head stone with Grandmother Lettie's name on it."

"Mom had driven herself uptown and Aunt Nancy and Aunt Hattie E took Billy and me up there to find her."

"After Grandmother Lettie died, I knew we were in big trouble." Mom asked Granddaddy George and 'Queen Esther' if Billy and I could stay with them until she came back to get us.

"Neither Billy nor I wanted to stay at Granddaddy George's house. It appeared that THE QUEEN ESTHER had moved in with Granddaddy George and my two aunts. She was always over there. Then they got married, or so they said."

We saw how she was treating Aunt Nancy and Aunt Hattie. After a week, Mom left Granddaddy's house.

They began hearing Queen Esther telling on them.

"They're lazy as 'all get- out', Esther told Granddaddy George."

She wasn't whispering. She wanted us to hear her.

"Queen Esther had become Mary and Billy's abuser."

Mary's outlet was reading and studying.

Mary said "I wouldn't call Esther by name because I didn't want to call her 'Grandmom Esther'.

She was the wicked step-Grandmom to me. Billy called her Grandmom and she treated him better.

"I called her "Queen Esther, to myself but let it slip out loud one day. That's when Esther told Granddaddy George on me."

BIODIVERSITY MATTERS

"There was another dilemma or predicament between Billy and me. Billy was light-complexioned and I was dark complexioned. Esther liked Billy better because she was light-skinned, also."

"Skin coloring mattered a lot in that house and in that little town that we all grew up in."

Mary said, "People were always comparing me to Billy when they saw us together. Neither of us liked that. We were close, born one year apart.

I had heard some of the school children call Billy and me 'Mutt and Jeff, or "Caulk and Charcoal," said Mary. It made us both feel bad and unaccepted. When we were young, even the adults called it teasing. They two called us names and laughed at Billy and me.

Today, that type of taunting is called bullying and is not tolerated by society. We felt rejected and isolated from the other children in school. We didn't know them well. We would come back to Delaware in the middle of a school year and there were always new children or teenagers in our class room.

"We could not help our genes. Billy had blond, straight hair and hazel green eyes. He was skinny, yet very handsome." He looked just like his daddy Willie, except Willie was darker. Willie's mother was very fair-complexion. That's where Billy got his fair complexion from, both of his grandmothers. Grandmother Lettie was very fair complexioned and my step-daddy, Willie's mother was very fair complexioned.

"I don't know where Billy got his blond, straight hair and hazel green eyes. He must have dug way back in the genes for those features. No one else in our immediate family had blond hair and green eyes," Mary said.

Mary stated, "I remember talking to Bertrand, II my young cousin, when he was with you. You came to my house and we were chatting about Billy who had recently died. (This was after all the cousins were grown and had their own families.)

Bertrand, II told Mary, "Billy, your brother is my first cousin just as you are. Billy had blond hair and green eyes. My second daughter, Kiara, has blond hair and brown eyes. Kiara's mother has hazel eyes and brown hair. I have cold black hair and Mother (Marian) said I had blue eyes when I was born. My eyes are brown, now."

"We call that biodiversity," said Bertrand, II. We don't know how far back our features and our children's features go."

"We need to get a fuller understanding about biodiversity. We used to call Billie a 'throwback' when I was younger," I said.

"When a child used to not look like either parent but have features like a grandparent or a great- grandparent, the old folk called him or her a 'throw back.' The child's genetic pool reached back to the ancestors."

"So here goes," Bertrand, II said. Bertrand II came back into the den with facts on Biodiversity and Human Well-Being.

He said, "My source is Copyright @ GreenFacts 2001-2018, a registered trademark of Cogeneris Spri. Design: Morris & Chapman."

Mary said, "With all my reading, it takes a science person a chemist, to teach me some new facts."

Bertrand II said, "Ok, guys, there's a lot to it. I'll just give you one generalized statement about biodiversity."

"Biodiversity is the viability among living organisms from all sources including the ecological complexes of which they are a part; this includes diversity within the species and between the species.

"So, there are two blond haired members in our immediate family, Mary. Your brother, Billy Pepper and your first cousin, Bertrand Griffin, II's daughter, Kiara Griffin. The other sides of your brother's ancestors and the other sides of Kiara's family apparently had blond hair and green/brown eyes and are very fair complexion. We do know from sight that someone in both sides of our families had blond hair and green/blue/brown eyes," I said.

"We used to call Billy 'Little Blondie.'

Mother Lettie didn't like for us to call Billy, 'Little Blondie'. She would say, "You have already nick-named the child, Billy. His real name is Willie Alex Pepper, after his father. That's enough nick-name," Mother would say.

Bertrand, II said "Let' get back to facts about biodiversity."

"No feature on earth is more complex, dynamic and varied than the layers of living organisms. Millions of species including humans have experienced dramatic changes within the ecosystem and at the hands of humans with these extraordinary, singularly unique features on earth and yet have thrived."

"There is so much to biodiversity that it bears a more thorough research and discussion than we can deal with now," Bertrand, II said.

"I tried to paraphrase and condense the material my source gave me. I have been interested in this subject since I was a kid. I just didn't know what I was looking for. When Mom (Marian). bought two sets of Encyclopedia, I was little. I would take two at a time and read up into the night. That was my hobby. Little did I know then that I would need this information and I always wanted to know more," Bertrand, II said.

Mary said, "Boy, am I glad you-all stopped by my house on your way to Delaware. (Mary now lives in South Carolina.)

Mary said, "Billie's first son, Arshawon Brown, born January 29, 1977, is fair complexion and looks just like him. His other four children varied in skin coloring: Tikia, Lentia, Willie and Jermaine Brown They were all born in Delaware. Billie wife was Terri Brown. (Billie is deceased.}

Mary said, "I have dark brown- complexion, dark brown eyes; I am big boned and have a head full of nappy, wooly hair. I would sneak and try to straighten my hair when Queen Esther and Granddaddy George left the house. I had to be careful and try to figure out if they would be gone for a long time. I didn't want them to smell the hair smoke and get to fussing. I had to always be on guard, taking care not to get caught doing something wrong."

I didn't have any hair grease to put on my hair so I used lard out of the pantry. I got good at straightening my hair so I felt better. I went to school with a little more self-confidence.

"Billy was just about in the same boat as I was, no decent clothes. He did not like school anyway. He quit school in tenth grade and started working in the fields or where ever he could find a job. Our Grandpop George and 'Queen' Esther liked the fact that he quit school. They demanded money from him. They didn't even realize that Billy was traumatized by all the abuse we had experienced as children. They didn't care."

The Heath house was just a place to sleep. Billy and I stayed away from home or outside as much as possible.

"We didn't know where our parents were. We learned from Granddaddy George that they had separated and had to go to divorce court. Granddaddy

George had to take us to court. The court asked us which parent we wanted to stay with. Quite naturally, I replied, "I want to be with my mom."

Billy said, "I will go with my dad."

Then Willie came to get Billy's clothes from Granddaddy George's house. He happily went with his daddy. He, too, was tired of living with 'Queen Esther' and our docile Granddaddy George.

"Mom took me to the state of Virginia with her for a short period in the summer-time and brought me back in the Fall so that I could return to high school in Bridgeville, Delaware."

"The only thing, after Billy left and Mom left, I was on my own. My two aunts, Nancy and Hattie E had finished high school and started to college. My uncles, Uncle George, Daniel and Joseph were all in the Navy. Aunt Marian had left years ago to go to graduate school and I hadn't seen her for a long time."

"I had no one in the Heath household to rely on. I knew I was in big trouble. I had one more year in high school, my senior year. I was determined to make it and graduate from high school."

Tavis Smiley quoted motivational speaker, Les brown, in his book, FAIL UP.

Brown said, "When life knocks you down, try to land on your back, because if you can look up, you can get up." (p. 1.)

Smiley went on to say, "Failure is an inevitable part of the human journey. Fail up is the trampoline needed when you're down. When you take the time to learn your lessons, when you use those lessons as stepping- stones to climb even higher than you were before, you transcend failure – "you fail up."

Mary knew she was going to have a hard time, a rough row to hoe the last year in high school. No support what-so-ever!

When Grandmother Lettie was living, Mary was happy in the Heath home. Everyone was kind to her. She knew how to pray. Moreover, she learned the true meaning of prayer.

Mary went to church as much as she could. She had friends there, mostly smaller children and older adults. The people there were nice to her. Once and a while, one of the older ladies would slip Mary a quarter or a dollar so she could buy herself a sandwich or fruit.

We can always expect to have problems. But Mary had horrendous issues and struggles from an infant to her high school days. It was no surprise to Mary that she had to learn who she wasn't in order to embrace who she was.

Mary realized that each of us is created with innate gifts and a purpose in life. Jesus wanted her to spread all of her humility and creativity around and let her light shine. The world gets better when we step into what God has for us.

Mary found this passage of scripture in an old Bible an elderly fried gave her.

> "We have different gifts, according to the grace given to
> each of us.
> If your gift is prophesying, then prophesy in accordance
> with your faith.
> If it is serving, then serve, if it is teaching, then teach;
> If it is to encourage, then give encouragement,
> If it is giving, then give generously.
> If it is to lead, do it diligently.
> If it is to show mercy, do it cheerfully.
> (Romans 12:6-8, NIV.)

Mary struggled through living with two impossibly repulsive elderly persons. Seemingly, there was no connection between Mary and these two persons, even though Granddaddy George was her real grandfather. He just listened to and catered to "Queen Esther."

Many African American families suffered the effects of life's uncertainties.

Jesus, in His sermon on the Mount said, "Blessed are the poor in spirit, for theirs is the Kingdom of heaven." (Matthew 5: 3, NIV.)

Mary said, "Sometimes I looked at my life and asked myself if my weaknesses were an opportunity for God's power to be made perfect in me. Did I really accept His grace as sufficient in all my situations? I was growing up fast."

Mary told me, "With all my reading, I read the Bible every day. I remember reading about Paul having a thorn in the flesh and asking, no begging God to remove it. God responded not by removing the agonizing source of pain but by giving Paul the strength to bear it." (2 Corinthians 12: 7-9, NIV.)

"This is how God often works," I said.

"He doesn't remove the splinter but He gives us the strength and power to conquer it."

Mary checked some of the places where they used to live. She got in touch with her mother, Phyllis when she graduated from high school. Phyllis was able to come and see her daughter march across that stage. They were both happy that day. Phyllis had hopes that her family would still succeed through Mary Drucilla.

Just before Mary graduated, the high school counselor called Mary into her office. She suggested that Mary go to college. Her grades were the best in the school. She had all A's except one B.

Mary thought she would like college. It would give her the chance to get out of Granddaddy George's house.

CHAPTER III

Mary Drucilla's College Days at Howard University

Mary selected Howard University because this was the University that Aunt Hattie E was attending. She could stay with her.

Mary received a scholarship to attend Howard University in Washington, D.C. She was told by the high school counselor that she had performed well on her SAT tests and had very good grades.

The white counselor did not show Mary her grades or her SAT score. She just informed her that she did well. Mary accepted this and went away happy that she might get to go to college.

Later, Mary told me that she was happy that she qualified to go to college because her Mom didn't graduate from high school.

"Mary," I said, "your mother did graduate from high school. She just did not march across the stage because she sassed her senior advisor the day of graduation. Mrs. Dixon told her she wouldn't walk across the stage and graduate with her class."

Your Grandparents, Lettie and George took Phyllis and all of us back to school that night to see Phyllis graduate. She went into the school to practice her graduation march. She came right on back out and told our parents that she was not graduating.

Mother Lettie went into the school and found out that Phyllis had the grades and number of courses to graduate but her senior class advisor had flagged her not to march, because Phyllis had been very rude and said a cuss word in front of her. She told Phyllis not to come to graduation. But she came anyway and brought her whole family thinking that she could 'bull doze' the advisor.

Mary said, "All these years, Mom thought she hadn't graduated from High school. She ran away from home and stayed with her Uncle Leon in Philadelphia. Then she moved in with Aunt Mary Paulson."

Moreover, years later, Mary graduated and her mother, Phyllis attended her graduation. Mary didn't attend the same high school as her mother.

She was sent to college on scholarship. Hattie E was attending Howard U. Her field of study was nursing. Mary moved in with Hattie E and Hattie's small daughter, Crystal.

Hattie E had a small apartment and was happy to let Mary stay with her.

Mary did very well in high school, graduated with the highest honors in her class, and received a scholarship to attend college. Mary made the valediction speech. Her advisor assisted her in writing it. She was so spellbound, she could hardly talk. Everyone praised her and said that she did a beautiful job.

Phyllis took Mary to Washington D. C. to attend Howard University. She would stay with Hattie E and Crystal, her little cousin.

At first, when Mary got to Howard University, she did not do well. She found out that being right was not nearly as important as being in a right relationship with others. She still had a very low self-esteem. She had not really learned to love herself.

"Love your neighbor as yourself. Love does no harm to its neighbor. Therefore, love is the fulfillment of the law. (Romans13:10, NIV.)

Tavis Smiley said it best. "My peers in college had no idea that I was fighting an inner battle against race and poverty, based on low self-esteem. They didn't know that I was trying to prove that I was the greatest, having the arrogance of youth." (p.3.)

That pretty much sums it up for Mary, too.

Smiley was trying to pattern his life after Muhammad Ali. Ali was arrogant. I was attempting to prove that I was the greatest also. Ali's razzle-dazzle poetic slings and barbs defeated his opponents as much as the physical scars he left. Ali heaped dishonor and disgrace on the hard-hitting take on prisoners Philadelphia brawler with his words:

"Frazer is so ugly that he should donate his face to the United States Bureau of Wildlife.

"It's gonna be a thrilla, and a chilla, and a killa when I get the Gorilla in Manila."

Even though Ali gave Frazier some of the most chilling unnecessary, below the verbal blows, "Frazier realized that they needed each other to produce some of the greatest fights of all times." (p.5.)

"Throughout his career, Muhammad Ali used his mouth and in-your-face tactics to force his way back into boxing, after being put out and exiled from boxing when he refused to fight in the Vietnam war. He was a Muslim and changed his name from Cassius Clay to Muhammad Ali. He may have been forcing himself to prove that he could overcome obstacles that no other boxer had ever had to contend with." (p.5.)

Mary had been isolated and lonely for so long, she couldn't identify herself or what her talents were. She didn't know what her purpose in life was. She had learned to pray at an early age. It was time for her to pull out that knowledge again and get to praying. She sometimes read her old Bible.

She became self-critical and began finding fault in her character, her physical appearance and her behavior. She began acknowledging her shortcomings, reaching unnecessary and inaccurate conclusions about herself.

Mary had such negative and self- loathing thoughts about herself.

She began praying about her 'hurt feelings and emotional pain to try and minimize the damage to her self-esteem.

In order to avoid kicking ourselves when we are down, we have to be able to 'argue' with our self-critical voice and adopt a kinder perspective. "(Winch. P. 18.)

We each have different gifts according to the grace given to each of us. (Romans12: 6, NIV.)

We have to learn to be self-supportive and embrace who we are, because we are each created with innate abilities and a purpose.

Susanna Foth Aughtmen stated in MORNING WITH JESUS, "God wants us to spread all that light and creativity around. We need each other's brightness and beauty." (p,2)

Mary loss all her steam when she got to college.

Mary said, "I was afraid to live. My life was changing before my eyes."

Her first day of class was traumatic. She attempted to catch a city bus from Hattie E's apartment to the Howard University campus. As she got on the bus, she became frightened and turned and got back off. She walked to school. By the time she got there, she had missed the orientation session for new freshmen.

Day after day, she went to class but would stand outside the class room doors, afraid to enter the class rooms. She felt at risk, frightened to sit in class with such beautiful renowned people. She did not do well her first semester. She was informed that she was on probation toward the end of the first semester.

CHAPTER IV

Mary Drucilla's Attempted Suicide

When Mary got her probation letter, she felt so desponded and depressed. She was still living with Hattie E and Crystal. She went home to the apartment and found some of Hattie E's medicine in the cabinet. There was a whole package of large pills in the cabinet. Mary took a large glass of water, went into her room and took the pills. Then she laid down and crossed her arms over her chest. She dosed off but woke back up. She had not died.

She realized that it was time to go pick Crystal up from the school bus. Crystal was attending Nursery school and Mary was a big help to Hattie E in picking Crystal up.

Mary mused, "I wonder why I didn't die? Why did my suicide attempt fail?"

She told Hattie E about the attempt about a week later. Hattie, a nursing student at Howard University, had brought home a large package of cough drops for her sore throat. They laughed and laughed about that incident.

At the end of the semester, Mary went home to Delaware. By this time, Phyllis, Mary's mother was living and working in Delaware. Mary got a job and worked during the school break. She decided to return to Howard University; her mother took her back to school. Hattie E suggested that she live on the campus the second semester. Mary moved into a resident hall.

She had a roommate from Peru who introduced her to a handsome young man from an Island.

The second semester, her grades were much better. She improved her habits of studying and reading. At the same time, Mary met someone who made her feel good about herself. You can't just rely on someone else to make you feel good. You have to gain self- assurance in your own skin.

However, Mary fell in love and was reassured that this young man from the West Indies felt the same way.

"You look just like my grandmother," he said, when he was introduced to her. He was not a student at Howard University, also. He worked at an industrial plant in Washington.

The internationally acclaimed poet, Maya Angelou, said in her book, THE HEART OF A WOMAN, "I've learned that people will forget what you said, people will forget what you did, but people will never forget how you made them feel."

Mary would smile at him whenever he came near her. She asked him one day which Island he was from.

"Just West India," he replied. "It's a beautiful place. I'd like to take you there sometime."

They started dating, meeting after Mary's classes and going to lunch or dinner together.

Finally, they started dating off campus. Things were working out very fine. Mary would come back to her residence hall and see this young man waiting for her.

She was adjusting to college life. Through all of the hurt and pain, Mary, a nineteen- year- old young lady began to up her self-esteem.

As Sarah Smarsh said in her book, HEARTLAND, "I felt large in my own skin but small beneath the black sky. I felt young and old at the same time." (p.248.)

"I knew struggles along highways as a way of life and immediately felt that I could identify with the many women who had horrific challenges. (para. p, 251.)

Later, Mary and I continued our discussion of her past.

"History is written by the victors, Mary. You have written your own history and you are continuing to turn the pages," I told her.

Somewhere along the line, I used to think that I was making wrong decisions and wrong choices. Growing up, I didn't know how to change my path and was running in several different directions," said Mary. Now I know, God is a forgiving God. He helps us to overcome any obstacle that prevents us from heading in the right direction."

Mary decided to enlist in the Navy after her second year at Howard University.

CHAPTER V

Mary Drucilla's Navy & Marriage Years

Dave was pressing Mary to get married. He seemed very anxious to start a life with her.

Mary moved from Hattie E apartment and lived in a residence hall the second semester with a roommate room Peru. She finished that semester and made all A's.

Mary got back on track with her studies but did not have enough money to return to college the next semester. She considered attending the police academy but changed her mind about that venture.

Mary decided to enlist in the Navy and did her basic training. This was one of the hardest things she had ever done. She got through it with encouragement from two of her uncles- George and Daniel.

Then Dave, the man who courted her in Washington, D. C. encouraged Mary to marry him. Dave and Mary got married. They were not doing well financially at first because Mary was just coming out of basic training and Dave had a menial job.

Mary moved to Texas and was stationed in Kingsville, Texas on her first ship. She had her first child, Dereka there. Dave, her husband, flew to Kingsville during that time. He stayed in Texas for about three weeks with Mary and Dereka, then returned to Washington, D.C. The couple got along fine when they were not under the same roof together.

Mary wanted her family to be together and she wanted more children. When Dereka was two years old, Dave flew down to Kingsville, Texas to help Mary move back to Washington, D.C.

The young family stopped in Baton Rouge and stayed with the Griffin family for two weeks. Mary re-enlisted into the Navy and trained for a different career. Mary was working in her field in the Navy and Dave was working in computer science field.

They were comfortable and happy together.

A.J. Russell said in his book, GOD CALLING, "What greater treasures can you have than peace, rest and joy; but all of these things are stolen from you by doubt, fear and despair." (p.103.)

Their marriage was turned around when they placed their two and a half-year-old daughter, Dereka in a nursery. Mary was taking a bus back and forth to her Naval station. She was taking Dereka to nursery school in the morning before she went to work. Dave was driving her car to his work. He was supposed to pick Dereka up from the nursery school each evening. His work schedule was more flexible than Mary's was.

Sometimes he didn't pick their child up. Mary would get a call from the nursery that Dereka was still there. Mary had to take the bus to the nursery from her job in the evening and catch another bus home with their child.

CHAPTER VI

Mary Drucilla's Failed Marriage

Mary and Dave began arguing over this issue and other issues. Dave thought that Mary was making too many demands on him. A baby is the woman's responsibility from his perspective.

Mary was pregnant again at the time. She was still in the Navy. She realized that he was staying away from home more and more. She had to face the fact that he was living with someone else.

Christina G, Hibbert, in her book WHO AM I WITHOUT YOU? said, "It takes two to make a marriage work."

She said, "I did everything to save our marriage because I thought of my two children being children of a divorce and the idea of a single parent was guilt-inducing, terrifying and incredibly saddening." (p.2.)

"Dave was acting more and more like a child. He wanted his own way all the time. Each attempt to save our marriage was unsuccessful and was at the expense of my own well-being, Including 'reconciling' three times." (p.1.)

Mary had her second child, Andrew. She was quite happy and content for a brief while. She had a period of rest from being in the Navy and having her second child.

She thought, "It is possible to discover her self- worth which would lead to a healthier relationship down the road. Her self-esteem increased and "she began to enjoy all the benefits of living a life of confidence, hope and love." (p. 2.)

Dave was staying home more and seemed a little more attentive. Some might call this time a 'my peace-at-any-price' groveling time." (p.v.)

Dave was thrilled to have a son. He would sit and hold his son, Andrew. Andrew was a beautiful baby and would look at Dave adoringly. He would feed and change Andrew. Mary didn't have that kind of help with Derika because Mary was in Texas alone with Dereka.

Mary said, "Then I realized that the bills were not being paid by my husband. We were getting 'late' notices. I paid my own bills when I was in Kingsville, Texas and when I first came to Washington, D. C.

They had a joint account but Dave was managing the money at that time. He started arguments, and when she answered him, he would become violent and abusive. Mary finally left one night and took her two children with her. She didn't have anywhere to go, so she went to a half-way house and was given a small room with one bed in it. She and her children slept together.

She cried and cried and her children cried.

Mary cried from relief and blessedness of being away from an abusive husband.

"You're going to have ups and downs. That's a part of overcoming a breakup, that's a part of developing unwavering self-esteem and learning to love again. Get back up again," said Hibbert. (p. 3.)

"Obstacles began to build back up; obviously, these were difficult times" said Mary.

Hatefulness and evil don't need any extra condemnation. Its evil speaks for itself.

"When we got an eviction notice to move out of our apartment, Dave left the apartment and stayed gone for several weeks. Then he came back and got his clothes. His clothes were mostly new. He had been buying new clothes with all of our money," Mary said. That's when we had our big blow-out and I knew our marriage was over.

Mary thought back to three years ago. "Didn't we promise to love and comfort each other, for better, for worse, for richer or poorer, in sickness and in health for as long as we both shall live?"

"When we lovingly answered "I do", it was hard to imagine what day-to day life would look like. We had been married for only a short period of time. I realized that marriage takes a lot of hard work and understanding. Even in the healthiest, happiest of marriages, obstacles and hard feelings would occur. Arguments would crop up."

"I began being angry all the time. Everything going on in our marriage was affecting our children. They were crying and sickly all the time. I knew things had to change."

"Whenever Dave came home, he started an argument. He 'hit below the belt.' I didn't have the kind of words in my vocabulary that he threw at me. He said hurtful things, while I tried to remain respectful."

'Bringing up things that were sensitive, name calling, saying things about my looks and my color should have been off limits, but they were the order of the day."

Mary went to the bank the day she got paid from the Navy to get money to pay the rent and it was all gone. Mary knew she was in big trouble.

Mary mused, "I found myself staggering through the wreckage of a failed marriage and the disintegration of my life as I knew it. Our marriage was beyond repair. The betrayal of my husband was devastating. I was using denial to protect myself."

"It finally dawned on me that Dave never loved me. He used me to get a green card and residency to the United States from his West India Island," Mary said.

"For the longest time, he wouldn't even tell me which island he was from. By the time he told me, I didn't care."

Winch said, "The urge to be self- critical in such situations can be extremely powerful. To win this internal debate, we need talking points, arguments we can use to formulate a more balanced understanding of why things occurred like this." (p. 18.)

Before we make plans for a new day, we would do well to engage in self-evaluation.

Hibbert said, "As much as we wish for an easier path to personal growth, the most effective one often seems to be paved with heartache, despair and fears that throw us unceremoniously to our knees."

Mary told me, "While some breakthroughs and enlightenments may come softly and quietly, in bite -size pieces, our marriage was doomed and I learned from the impetus of pain and loss."

Mary said, "I borrowed money from several family members and moved to another apartment with my children. Dave moved back in with me and the children. Mary learned that Dave was cheating on her and was living with a white woman. He was very fair- complexion and was from a West India Island. He could live in a white neighborhood."

Mary told me, "He was back and forth from my apartment to his white girlfriend's apartment." Whenever he came to my apartment, he would start an argument and walk out. He was having it both ways."

Mary found out that he was using the girlfriend by telling her he needed to sleepover because his wife had put him out of their apartment.

One day Mary gleaned that the arguments were started so that he could leave. Mary started divorce proceeding. She had gotten fed up with his demeaning ways. She had tried her best to keep it all together for the sake of her children. She didn't want them to be fatherless as she and her brother, Billy were when their mother left their father and moved back in with different relatives.

Mary said, "Dave used verbal abusive and crude language such as name -calling and racial slurs to upset me. My children were constantly crying. In his country, he was considered white and he wanted to be with white people. I was very dark."

"I was seriously going through bouts of brokenness and pain, insecurity and self-hate. I even got out of the Navy because of his taunting and abuse. My self-esteem was very low. I just wanted to escape and flee from the bitterness and heartache," Mary said.

"My husband had deserted his family but I didn't want to believe it."

Dave did not want a divorce. He was on Mary's health insurance and life insurance. It was the best insurance and he had dropped his insurance and was no longer paying for it. So, Dave did not want to lose his coverage.

Also, Mary had re-enlisted in the Navy, moved up in rank in the Navy and was making more money than Dave. He did not want to lose his added income, either.

"Getting a divorce would not be a 'win' for him. He was having it his way, both ways, but he wouldn't do right so he wasn't winning," Mary said.

Mary left Washington and went to Delaware to stay with her mother, Phyllis for a short period of time. Her children and she were very unhappy there. Old memories returned about her childhood.

Guy Winch, in his book, EMOTIONAL FIRST AID, said, "One of the reasons our self-esteem is so vulnerable and fragile is because we don't feel accepted by others." (p. 13.)

"She remembered her family constantly moving and her step-father trailing behind them. Her mother could get a job wherever they moved. Willie, her step -father was always without work. That's why he came back to them to have a livelihood without earning it."

Mary and her mother had married the same type of men, lazy, abusive and unsupportive.

"When our need to belong remains unsatisfied for extended periods of time, either because of the rejection we've experienced or because we lack the opportunity to create supportive relationships, it can have a powerful and detrimental effect on our psychological and physical health," (Winch, p.13.)

She had also left the Navy and didn't have money to support herself and her children.

While at her mother's house, Mary became ill with her childhood memories of always moving from one state to another, from one relative to another.

She thought, "Are my children and I going to be nomadic and traumatized like I was as a child. She had read when she was in high school, that her ancestors from Africa were nomadic.

Mary read that African American's genealogies were at best fractured and dismembered due to separations of families through slavery and other tragedies. Dis-functional families caused strife and heartache.

When she left Dave for good, he was very angry. His 'bread and butter' was leaving him.

Mary said, "I took my children and moved in with my mother's trailer in a small town in Delaware until I could get up enough nerve and stamina to ask for help from someone else."

"I went to Nancy and Albert Kellam, my aunt and uncle, in Seaford, Delaware and they allowed us to move in with them without much fanfare. We felt welcome there"

CHAPTER VII

Mary Drucilla's Reenlistment in the Navy

Mary was in and out of the Navy. She decided to re-enlist again. She went on a diet and loss a lot of weight and re-enlisted. This time, she wanted to stay in until she could retire. She also wanted to go back to college and finish her degree. She left Delaware and took her children with her.

She trained for another career in the Navy and left her children with a good friend who cared for them for two years.

Then she realized that she would be away from her children for longer periods of time and decided to leave the children with Uncle George Heath, Jr. who was still in the Navy himself. He and his family lived near Norfolk; Virginia as George had been stationed there for years at the Naval Base.

This was working out fine. George, Jr.'s wife was caring for the children and Mary was paying her monthly. Ultimately, Aunt Corrine became ill and there were gaps in the care of Mary's children.

Even though she was very worried and concerned about her two children, Mary needed time away from it all. She needed time to herself to heal from her many unhealthy relationships, especially her husband, Dave. She could not get clear of grieve and pain, and re-discover who she really was until she stopped 'see-sawing with her ex. She needed time to overcome, become and flourish in order to regain self-worth again and accept what had happened to her.

Mary explained to me, "I had to get over the guilt feelings of leaving my children with other families; but the Navy was the only source I knew to make a decent living. I didn't enjoy the way I was living, away from my children.

I didn't want to accept how I had been treated or what I had been through; but I had to accept the way things were and move on."

"Mary mused, "I began praying in earnest. Thinking 'if I pray to do what God wants me to do, He will change my life. I was still a relatively young person. I began to think like an adult, more rationally. I had the benefit of hindsight, knowing what really happened to me."

According to Elizabeth Smart in her book, MY STORY, "There are examples of men in combat who have frozen with fear, unable to do the task they were trained to do. Sometimes they shut down, losing their ability to function in almost every way: mentally, emotionally and physically. (p. 36.)

"That is why their training is so important," Mary reiterated.

Mary got readjusted to her way of life in the Navy and after several years, she married a Navy man. She returned to Virginia to get her two children from Uncle George and Aunt Corrine's house. Her second husband was stationed in Washington State. She left her children with him and went back overseas.

Her children, Dereka and Andrew, were young teenagers by this time and could care for themselves. They could get to school and take care of the house.

Mary's younger cousin, Bertrand Griffin, II (who is our son) lived in Washington State and would visit Dereka and Andrew occasionally with his own family.

Bert, (my husband) and I flew out to Washington State to visit Bertrand, II's family and Mary's family. The two families were thriving and helping each other. The two children were trying to heal from the brokenness from the break-up of their parents.

Dereka was doing well in high school. However, Andrew was not doing as well. He didn't like school. He was stubborn and wanted to go back to his father, Dave, who still lived in Washington, D.C.

Dave allowed Andrew to stay with him for about a week and then sent him home. Andrew was frustrated and disillusioned. He thought he could live with his father for the rest of his life. He had always been close to his father when he was a small child.

Dave had moved on. He had a new family, now; 'no room in the inn' for Andrew.

Andrew returned to Washington State to live with his step-father, James, who was his mother's second husband. Andrew started acting out, being rude and disobedient. The only person he felt he could turn to was Dereka, his older sister.

Andrew began writing to his mother, telling her how dissatisfied and disappointed he was with his living conditions.

Mary came home as soon as she could to help Andrew. After a while, she was able to relocate in the Navy. Her whole family moved to South Carolina. Both parents were still in the Navy.

Helen Keller once said, "Alone we can do so little; together we can do so much."

Mary related to me, "My relationship with my second husband was good, but we had differences of opinion about certain things, including how to clean the house. During our marriage, we had not gotten the opportunity to live in the same house or apartment for a long period of time because we were stationed in different areas of the world."

"When I got to South Carolina, James was living in a house he was planning to buy and live in after he retired. He was very meticulous and approached the upkeep of 'his' house in his own style. I couldn't keep up with him.

I began praying and asking God for strength and encouragement to raise my family as well as merge the two families. Eventually as I scrutinized his style of keeping house, I had to change my perspective and accept the differences that got the same results."

I cried out, "I am slipping!" but Your unfailing love, O Lord, supported me. When doubts filled my mind, Your comfort gave me renewed hope and cheer. (Psalm 94: 18-19, NLT.)

"I felt strange in his house because we had not selected the house together, and I had to restrict my children from doing things in the house. Also, he had two children by a previous marriage and they visited him regularly.

Conditions are rarely perfect, but James respected me and my children.

"It was up to me to learn the same. James cared for my children and looked out for them because I was out at sea more often than he was. Oftentimes he had two sets of children in his home. Sometimes that is an impossibility."

"Jesus looked at his disciples and said, "With man, this is impossible, but with God all things are possible." (Matthew 19: 26, NIV.)

Jesus had the ability to make something out of nothing, to see impossibilities and turn them into answers.

"As for me, since I am poor and needy, let the Lord keep me in His thoughts. You are my helper and my savior. O my God, do not delay," (Psalm 40: 17, NLT.)

Evan though, James and Mary had a lot in common, their marriage did not work out.

They both had too much baggage and confusion in their lives. They both retired from the Navy after twenty- one and a half -years of service.

They both bought separate homes and remained friends.

Eleanor

Mary Heath Cherry

George HEATH, Sr.
B: 12/31/1910

Lettie HARPER HEATH
B: 12/07/1908
D: 1/30/1961

Rev. Bertrand Griffin, I Nancy Heath Kellam

Joseph B. and Barbara D. Heath

Nancy Heath Kellam and Albert Lee Kellam, Jr.

Marian Olivia HEATH
b: 08/29/1939 in Delaware
B: 08/29/1939

Gloria Heath Martin

Gloria Heath Martin

Karen Griffin Phenix

Family of NATHANIEL STEVEN

Nathaniel HEATH
B: abt 1925

Marian Heath Griffin   Rev. Bertrand Griffin, I

Family of *MARY ETTA*

Mary E. HEATH
B: 1915

Elmer Poulson

Mary Heath Cherry graduation at University of S.C.

Preachers Children

Rev, J.C. Miles

Bertrand GRIFFIN, Sr.
B: 08/03/1934

CHAPTER VIII

Mary Drucilla's New College Life

When Mary needed strength, she turned to God, she prayed.

Nothing is coincidental. She was looking in a library near her new home in South Carolina.

She found something in a book, YESTERDAY, I CRIED BY Iyanla Vanzant. The words fit Mary's mood perfectly.

"I cried yesterday. I cried when I was a child. I cried when I was a teenager. I cried when I was a young woman. And it is the fear, the shame, and the pain of those tears that have allowed me to stand up today and tell my story, to tell my story and celebrate my healing. This is not just my story; it is our story."

It is the story of the common things that we experience, that we have not learned to express." (p. 27.)

Mary whispered to herself: "I've found my new best friend. I've found another human being just like me."

Vanzant goes on to say," This is the story that keeps us crippled because we hold our emotions down in fear, in anger, in shame. My prayer is that my story will help people throw away their crutches of dysfunction and addiction, (yes, allowing abuse is an addiction), so that we can all stand together in a new time, a new place, with a new understanding that enables us to celebrate the fact that we are still alive." (p. 27.)

Mary got out of her chair, walked to her door and opened it and went to Limestone College in Charleston, South Carolina, enrolled and completed her Bachelor's Degree in social work.

Then on to the University of South Carolina in Columbia, she enrolled there and received her Master's degree in the School of Social Work.

"Remembering what had happened to me at Howard University where I was frightened to death to go in the door of the University, I stood, broken; I bowed my head in prayer."

"I needed Jesus' attention and help. I begged Him for wisdom and perseverance -and actual tangible assistance."

"Glancing around me, I saw no one, she said.

"I put one foot ahead of the other."

My thoughts were, "I survived a broken abusive childhood, shameful teen years and a horrible marriage. I stayed twenty-one and a half years in the Navy working with mostly unruly white men. I was their supervisor. I was able to complete a Bachelor's degree.

"I am still in the Navy Reserve. I have served my country and will still serve it until the day I die. I could be called back into the Navy at any time, if I were needed."

"I am trying to get into a white university for a Master's degree in a highly prejudice state, South Carolina."

"Going into the university administration building, I realized that I had anxiety and fear. But then, anxiety and fear consume time, energy and emotions."

Jesus was constantly teaching, "Don't be anxious about your life" (Matthew 6:25, English Standard Version- ESV.)

"Jesus knew that we would be anxious about little things. He knew that we would be overly stressed and frantic, but even in the essential matters and issues of life, Jesus makes it clear that if we serve Him and trust Him, we should cross worrying off our list of problems."

"Jesus erases anxiety."

"Still a little nervous, I put my head up high," said Mary.

"I walked into the office and requested a registration package for the Fall semester."

"A chill ran through my body. The white lady at the desk didn't even look up or acknowledge me. She just reached down under her desk, retrieved a package and handed it to me. I said, "Thank you and left."

Mary said to herself, "You are going to have to love yourself and understand yourself before you can love others and understand others."

It was then and there that Mary decided to get her two degrees to help others in need. She felt her calling was to be a social worker. So, she wanted to receive her Master's degree in social work to help herself and others. She knew that she would have to make some great adjustments and work through the purpose in her life.

Mary's prayer was, "Give me more faith, God, in You and in myself."

"I can do all things through Christ who strengthens me," was her daily prayer.

God showed her a sign. "You've got to take the good times and the bad times and turn them into positives for yourself."

Mary registered that Fall in the school of social work and finished in two years. She had a year and a half of course credits from Howard University and more credit hours from classes taken in the Navy and Limestone College. She received her Bachelor's degree from Limestone College. Because she was continuing in the same major, she finished her Master's degree in social work in a year and a-half.

From the University of South Carolina. Mary sent her aunts and uncles and cousins invitations to her graduation.

"We came from New York, Delaware, Louisiana, Virginia, North Carolina, Texas as well as South Carolina and Georgia to her graduation. This was a special occasion for our family. Our first -born niece had finished two degrees in a short period of time," I said.

At the dinner party we gave Mary at a Hotel ballroom, Mary made a speech. "All of the women in my family went to college. All of the men went in the Navy or Army. I did both."

"I went to college. I went into the Navy, Then I went again to college and graduate school. I did both. I am so proud of myself."

"The next day, the whole family who had attended Mary's graduation, got on a cruise ship with Mary and took a cruise together."

"We celebrated my niece, Mary Drucilla."

CHAPTER IX

Mary Drucilla's Life After College

Life by no means was over for Mary, good or bad. Like a quilt, guilted from all fabrics of our lives, both beautiful and not so beautiful, it would multiple pieces to put our lives together. There were going to be many ups and downs continuing in her life. She may not have been the same person that she was a year ago, a week ago or when she was a child.

Mary Drucilla said, "Over the years, I sometimes felt a depression coming on, I felt like lying down and not getting up again. I came from a very humble beginning which left me ever so humble, but did not ultimately dictate the path I would take. Our circumstances may often present us with great challenges and hardships."

"I'll admit that my background gave me the gift of humility. Life is what you make it and how you live it."

Jesus said to his disciples, "I am the bread of life. He that cometh unto me shall never hunger, and he that believeth on me shall never thirst." (John 6: 35, KJV.)

Trip Lee, in his book, RISE, said, "Whatever it is you are doing, it is for God." (P. 73.)

"My life felt so much better. I am in control of my own destiny," Mary thought.

"Yet, experiences, good or bad, don't stop.

Winch said in his book, EMOTIONAL FIRST AID, "Once we have suffered profound and repeated rejection (and pain) over our lifetime, finding our place in the world and feeling as though we belong can be the hardest struggle of all." (p. 14.)

"Many of the rejections we face are significant and reoccurring. In such situations the risk of leaving our emotional wounds unattended can be profound. Not all rejections require first aid, but the survivor of the hurt and heartache does." (para. p.17.)

Mary said, "I didn't just have myself to deal with. I have two young adult children. That renders enormous consequences and challenges. We look at life differently when we have children. They are still growing and are very needy. What they lacked in their early childhood and teenage years is still waiting for me, their mother, to fulfill."

"They are having problems adjusting to life. They were insecure and unhappy when I was in the Navy, especially Andrew. He was constantly getting into trouble. As years went by, he seemed to trust only Dereka.

Mary did not know that Andrew was on drugs until she retired from the Navy. Everyone hid it from her. She did know that Andrew was in and out of school, had to repeat the ninth grade when he was fourteen years old. He went back to school when the family moved to a new city.

Mary realized that her son was starved for love, but she had no control over him. It was very upsetting to try and put your own life back together, only to actualize that your child is facing desperate insecurities and pain as well.

"Yet, we can rejoice in our sufferings, because we know that suffering produces perseverance; perseverance, character, and character, hope. And hope does not disappoint us, because God has poured out his love into our hearts by the Holy Spirit, whom He has given us." (Romans 5: 3-5, NIV.)

"Some of the experiences that I had as a young adult seemed trite in comparison to what Andrew was going through."

Mary became guilt-ridden and hurt. She blamed herself for Andrew's addiction. She had stayed away from him too long. He didn't like his step-father, James, and was disobedient to him. He was out of control as a teenager. He was smart but had very low self-esteem.

One day, Andrew went on a drug 'look-out' and got shot in the stomach. He remained in the hospital for several weeks, hanging on to a thread of his life. After the hospital stint, he went to prison for his deeds and dealing with drugs.

MARY DRUCILLA CRIED

Thinking that her life was going to be much better, Mary had to wonder, "When will the pain and suffering end.

Iyanla Vanzant, in her book, YESTERDAY, I CRIED, said, "The pain of the past does not have to be today's reality." {p. 21).

Mary said, "My children, a daughter and a son, that I wanted so badly, are causing me such heartache. Dereka got into a bad relationship with a young man and had to be rescued along with her infant son, Devonte."

"Andrew was following the drug scenes."

Mary acknowledged that she was a motherless child raising children. Even with her children around her, she once again felt the solitude and loneliness that the night brings.

Reading Iyanla Vanzant's book, YESTERDAY, I CRIED, Mary found clues to her own life.

Iyanla said, "She remembered the adults in her life who had taught her to be afraid., afraid of them and afraid of what they could do to her. She wrote about the pain that they had done and had not done. She remembered all the ways that they had hurt her body and her feelings. She thought about the things they had said and the lies they had told to her, on her and about her. She remembered how she trusted them to take care of her and protect her. They had not done that. People do not care about you." (Para. 153.)

Mary decided that she was not going to be like any of the adults who had raised her except Grandmother Lettie and her two young aunts, Nancy and Hattie E.

"After reading this book and other works by Vanzant, Mary recognized that she could pick herself up once more, write her feelings vicariously through a 'ghost writer' and move forward."

She told me, her aunt Marian, her story, because she knew I would write it for the edification of others.

Someone said:

"Every decision you make stems from what you think you are, and represents the value that you put upon yourself."

"You are unique unto yourself. No one else has your finger print. What you seek, seeks you," (para. p. 21.)

Jeremiah tells us that though we think we understand our hearts and minds, we can never fully understand ourselves or our motives. He went on to record, "I, the Lord search the heart and examine the mind." (Jeremiah 17:9, NIV.)

How you react or fail to react determines the course of your future."

"Just at the right time, when we were still powerless, Christ died for the ungodly; but God demonstrates His own love for us in this," (Romans 5: 6-8, NIV.)

PART TWO

CHAPTER X

Leslie Peter

Leslie Peter grew up in a preacher's home. He is a native of Bogalusa, Louisiana. He is a PK, preacher's kid. Dr. Norris is the son of Reverend Leslie Henry Peter Norris, Sr. and Mrs. Adele Washington Norris. Both parents are deceased.

Leslie Peter graduated from Southern University Laboratory High school, received his Bachelor of Arts degree from Southern University, Baton Rouge, Louisiana, His Master's degree in Education from Nicholls State University in Thibodaux, Louisiana and his Masters of divinity degree from Gammon Theological Seminary, Atlanta, Georgia.

For his service to the United Methodist church and society, a Doctor of Divinity degree was conferred on him by Gammon Theological Seminary of the Interdenominational Theological Center in Atlanta, Georgia.

Leslie Peter comes from a long line of preachers. His grandfather was an old country deacon/preacher, his father was a United Methodist preacher, his uncle was a United Methodist preacher (all deceased.)

Leslie Peter lost his father while he was in the seminary. Leslie experienced such grief and pain during that time. Rev. Leslie Henry Peter Norris, Jr was Leslie Peter's idol and hero. Dr. Leslie Henry Peter Norris, III was obviously named for his father.

Leslie Peter was very close to his father. Through his tears he realized that "God makes a way out of no way. He made Leslie Peter who he is because of his father on earth and his father who is in heaven.

Vanzant, in YESTERDAY, I CRIED, said, After all I had experienced and learned, I had to revisit my own past, which was filled with bitter tears in order to move into the future." (para. p. 14.)

"Sometime we are able to cry through the pain. Sometime we stumble through the pain. Sometimes we move through the pain in fear and anger without the strength to cry. When we do find our strength again, we move on to the next thing without taking a moment to breathe or celebrate." (p. 24.)

Leslie Peter has endured life's circumstances others cannot imagine and things others cannot understand.

Vanzant said it for Leslie Peter: "I cried because I hurt. I cried because hurt has no place to go except deeper into the pain that caused it in the first place, and when it gets there, the hurt wakes me up!" (Para. p. 18.)

Leslie Peter, through it all, has been available to help others and share whatever he has. He apparently has been on a soul search for God. Leslie learned through understanding and faith, that God existed in him."

"A prophet is not without honor, but among his own kin and in his own house." (Mark 6:4,KJV.)

"Jesus left there and went to his hometown, accompanied by his disciples. When the Sabbath came, he began to teach in the synagogue, and many who heard him were amazed.

"Where did this man get these things? What's this wisdom that has been given to him, that he even does miracles!

"Isn't this the carpenter's son? Isn't this Mary's son and the brother of James, Judas and Simon? Aren't his sisters here with us? And they took offense at him. (Mark 6: 1-3.NIV.)

Jesus said to them, "Only in his hometown, among his relatives and in his own house is a prophet without honor. He could not do any miracles there, except lay his hands on a few sick people and heal them. And he was amazed at their lack of faith." (Mark 6: 4-6, NIV.)

"If you strive against evil, no matter what the cost, righteousness is sure to triumph."

CHAPTER XI

Dr. Alfred L. Noris, Leslie Peter's Older Brother

Leslie Peter's older brother is a United Methodist minister of United Methodist churches, having served several large churches, served in the position as President of Gammon Theological Seminary of the Interdenominational Seminary Center, (both brothers attended Gammon), was appointed District Superintendent of the Louisiana Annual Conference, and became a dedicated Presiding Bishop of the United Methodist church.

HIS LOVE

Called to a new ministry. I travel there with joy,
I never know who I will find, but I'm in God's employ.
I cannot plan what there I'll do, or who I might there touch,
But I'm assured He'll be with me for He's my sturdy crutch.

Dr. Alfred L. Norris has held all of these titles, and many more in the United Methodist Church. Alfred is a dedicated family man, married to Mackie Norris, a Nurse Supervisor and two lovely children, who grew up to in the church and are leaders in their communities.

Can you imagine what a hard act that is to follow for Leslie Peter! Ancestral footsteps or foot prints and some broad shoulders to stand on.

Alfred L's philosophy is "If there is something in this world that does not exist, you must create it, that is, with the help of the Lord."

Deng Ming-Dao, in his narrative, LIVING WITH BALANCE AND HARMONY, as quoted in Vanzant's YESTERDAY, I CRIED:

"Life hurts. Life is painful. Life is suffering. There is nothing in life that does not involve trial."

"There is nothing worthwhile that doesn't have a cost. Yet, we must go on."

"There is nothing great that does not require a series of small acts. We must persevere. If we do, good times are sure to follow. If we constantly seek, even in darkness, guidance is sure to come." (p.19)

Alfred, too, is Leslie Peter's hero and big brother.

CHAPTER XII

Leslie Peter's Seminary Life

On his own, on his own ingenuity, Leslie Peter served in many capacities while at the Gammon Theological Seminary. He served internships at churches in Browning, Montana and its vicinity, attended the Mennonite Seminary as an exchange student, served an intern church in New York city and numerous churches in Atlanta, Georgia while still a student in Seminary.

Kevan Hart said in his book, I CAN'T MAKE THIS UP, "Life is a story full of chapters. And the beauty of life is that not only do you get to choose how you interpret each chapter, but your interpretation writes the next chapter. It determines whether it's comedy or tragedy, fairy tale or horror story, rags to riches or riches to rags." (p.7.)

"You can't always control the events that happen to you, but you can control your interpretation of them. So why not choose the story that serves you best." (p. 7.)

Leslie had a normal unassuming childhood except so much was expected of him. He grew up as a humble, courageous preacher's child. He was expected to do this and do that in the church. He received the call to preach at an early age, in his teens, though he may not have actualized it. He spoke well and sang with a beautiful tenor voice in the choirs of his father's churches from the time he was little.

Leslie learned a ton of things in his young life. He never faltered or failed, even though he sometimes became frustrated and fearful of making mistakes.

Marc Chernoff, in his book, GETTING BACK TO HAPPY, said, "You have to do hard things to be happy in life."

Oprah Winfrey said in LOVE YOUR LIFE, "The big secret in life is that there are no secrets. Whatever your goal, you can get there if you are willing to work."

I told Leslie Peter, "You cannot succeed alone. Your Creator is always there working in you and through you to accomplish what you set out to do. We all have defining moments in our lives. You have to fight to be triumphant over the ills and struggles of life and establish yourself. Let your work be your survival tool; survival with grace and faith."

Bertrand Griffin, Leslie Peter's 'roomie', says to him all the time, "You are still here, because God is not through with you yet. God still has work for you to do on earth." Be still and know that he is God!"

Jean Alerte remarked in his book, DO RIGHT DO GOOD, "Successful people like Leslie Peter are

only successful because of their continuous hard work and dedication in perfecting their crafts."

Everyone is working to get to the top, but where is the top? It's all about working harder and

getting better and moving up and up. The harder you work at something; you will get better at doing it" (p. 48.)

He said, "The things that most people avoid are those things that make them uncomfortable." (p. 49).

Kamala Harris said in her book, THE TRUTHS WE HOLD, "I believe there is no more important and consequential antidote for these times than a reciprocal relational of trust. You give and you receive trust. One of the most important ingredients in a relationship of trust is that we speak trust. It matters what you say. It matters what we mean. The value we place on our words- and what they are worth to others is most important." (para., p. xv).

I had heard of Leslie Peter from my husband, Bertrand. He told me that this young man was his roommate just before we got married.

Bertrand said, "He has a great sense of humor, is a smiling vivacious young man, but what is special about him is he is a very trustful, dedicated person and he is my friend."

I met Leslie Peter in one of my classes just after I married Bertrand Griffin and started attending Gammon Theological Seminary in Atlanta, Georgia.

Bertrand and Leslie had been roommates the year before. Leslie was teasing me, "telling me that I had taken his room -mate away from him."

Leslie Peter is a man of considerable strength and tenacity. "His natural courtesy saved him from enemies, while his fresh interest in others in life made his presence always agreeable."

"I realized that he is a prolific poet, producing an abundance of work or results. He accepts responsibility with a flair along with the splendor of living, the hope of a more heroic life."

So, Leslie Peter went his own way, had plenty of friends and always did a good job with whatever he undertook to do.

Leslie Peter went to school in Baton Rouge and New Orleans. He attended collage at Southern University, although he confided in me one day that "he wanted to attend Dillard University in New Orleans."

"My parents sent my older brother, Alfred to Dillard University and my parents sent me to Southern University. Dillard is a United Methodist University. That is why I wanted to attend there. We both attended the same seminary even though I went several years later then my older brother," Leslie said.

Leslie Peter spent most of his time as a youngster doing an amazing quality and quantity of work. What he sees and feels and knows, he gives to his fellowman.

He is a great story teller and began oral history about some of his experiences in life as a child and as an adult. One of his stories was an interesting one about an internship he had just completed that Summer in 1963.

He told me that he was glad that Bertrand had gotten married because he was always so quiet and seemingly lonely. Leslie and Bertrand were both from small towns in Louisiana, even though they did not really know each other before they met in Atlanta, Georgia to attend seminary.

They had seen each other one Summer when they attended Methodist Youth Camp in Waveland, Mississippi. Bertrand was in the older group because he was older than Leslie. So, there was not much interaction while they were there.

Leslie Peter caught up with Bertrand in school, because Bertrand went to Dillard University his freshman year, then left to enlist in the Air Force for three and a half years. After Bertrand left active duty in the Air Force, and became a reservist, he returned to Dillard and finished his undergraduate degree in two and a half years and received a Bachelor's degree in theology and philosophy.

The two young men became roommates as a result of both of them being from Louisiana.

I could tell that there was a special bond between Bertrand and Leslie Peter which materialized into their being best friends for life. Our families have merged, attending each other's children's debuts, weddings, and other special occasions.

Family and community are very important to both of them and it never ceases to amaze me that there were four families from Louisiana in Seminary together for three years. They came home to Louisiana and celebrated many holidays in each other's homes. Our children grew up together, attended high school together, even college together at Dillard University.

Most persons have very few good and special friends that last a life time as generations of children and grandchildren interact. Our families encouraged each other and shared resources with each other.

Each year these four ministers and their families met at United Methodist Conferences, luncheons, banquets, barbeques and the like. Our families continue to grow as a community. Our children grew up as a community. We love each other and are responsible for each other and everyone.

Our lives are intertwined and these ministerial lives have impacted many others lives in a positive way. Our families did not just have jobs. We had a collective ministry. This has been true with the hand of God working with and through them.

These four families were the Bertrand Griffin family, including Marian, wife and three children, Bertrand, II Karen Michelle, and Michael Gerard Griffin.

The Leslie H. Peter Norris family, including Roszeta, wife and two children, Leslie Peter, Jr. and Wendy;

The Robert Williams family, including Helen, wife (both deceased) and five children, Rolan, Mona, Deidre, Terry (deceased) and Sandra;

The Calvin family, including George W. C., and wife, May Calvin Belton, (both deceased) and three children, Charlotte, Bertina and George, Jr.

All four families graduated from universities in Louisiana and Gammon Theological Seminary of the Interdenominational Theological Center around the same time and moved back to Louisiana to become minsters in local churches.

CHAPTER XIII

Living and Working with
the Blackfoot Indians

Leslie Peter had a rich history of a missionary job reverted into his first year of his seminary study. He was so proud of his opportunity of having worked with this group of people.

"In the summer of 1963, The Methodist Board of Missions sent me, a seminary student, to Browning, Montana to do a pastoral internship at the Methodist Blackfoot Indian Mission," Leslie said.

"Shortly after my arrival in Browning, I was met by Rev. James Bell who outlined my summer ministry responsibilities. He spoke of the usual and the unusual. The most unusual was driving through the Rocky Mountains (void of guard rails) daily to visit twenty Blackfoot Indian homes."

"This was a tremendous challenge to me as I am accustomed to living and moving in the flatlands. In the flatlands, I felt comfortable and safe."

He didn't realize it, but he had apparently developed agoraphobia, which is a dread of open spaces or going out.

"I was generally anxious about life and my responsibilities. My sleep was erratic, my eating habits changed, I loss weight, I was a mess."

Leslie Peter said, "After leaving the mountainous area, driving with no guard rails, I had a sudden relief of being safe and secure again. Only to go day after day with the same routine!"

"Browning is surrounded by the Rocky Mountains and is near the Idaho and Canadian borders in northeastern Montana. The Blackfoot Indian Mission was led by a deeply committed and enthusiastic white missionary,

Rev James Bell of Methodism's Northwest Texas Conference. The Mission served Browning Methodist Church (comprised of white federal government employees and a smattering of half-blood Indians in Babb Methodist church in Babb, Montana, and Apistatake Methodist church in nearby Glacier National Park," Leslie Peter said.

"This area was inhabited by a small number of eighty to one hundred year- old full-blooded Indians who spoke no English, only a traditional Indian dialect," Leslie explained to me.

He continued, "There is a nearby United States Air Force Base Chapel. Rev, Bell served as part-time civilian chaplain. There were four churches in this area which were pastored every Sunday by Rev. Bell and me."

"Three white lay -persons were on our staff: Harry, a retired postal worker, Vicki, a college student from Missoula, Montana, and Holly, a college student from Chicago. These three lay persons were invaluable in performing non-ministerial duties."

Leslie explained this information to me when I first met him at the Interdenominational Theological Seminary (Gammon Theological Seminary) in Atlanta, Georgia. He had just written a report on his missionary experiences with the Blackfoot Indians and it was fresh on his mind. He was happy to have someone listen to him.

The first thing he said to me was, "Being right is not nearly as important as being in a right relationship with others."

He further indicated that Vicki, Holly and he resided in the Browning Methodist church parsonage with the Bell family: Rev. Bell, his wife and their two children of which one was a Blackfoot Indian child.

"He had to get adjusted to living with white people and working with Blackfoot Indians," he said.

Leslie Peter stated, "I was the only African American in Browning, other than Blacks who were forty miles away at the United States Air Force Base."

"On one occasion, the Mission staff joined several Blackfoot Indians in building a tepee and a camp fire within the tepee," he said.

"Leslie Peter reported that they all stayed in the Tepee overnight and the next day."

"I'm not a racist and this is the 1960's," Leslie told me at that time, "but it was a new experience for me. I had to stay grounded and humble. I had to focus on my purpose for being there."

"God had given me this great opportunity, this rich blessing and I am so thankful,"

"I prayed every night harder and harder."

"I sing praises to your name, for You are my rock."

"Up close and personal, I was using all my ingenuity to do what I was sent there to do,"

He said.

Alerte, in his book, DO RIGHT, BE RIGHT, said "I am convinced that many times in the course of our lives, the Creator challenges us to be more and more than what we thought possible."

"You are unique. No one suggested that you accept that challenge, by listening to the still voice within. You took the first step. What you seek, seeks you. So, now I challenge you."

"How you react or fail to react determines the course of your future. Trust me! Your faith will be rewarded." (p. 48).

Leslie Peter stated, "I was stunned at how Blackfoot Indians live. Most Blackfoot Indians live in huts with the ground as floors, no electricity, no plumbing, only outdoor toilets."

The Mission staff and Blackfoot Indians periodically joined several MYF Mission teams from Western states to improve dilapidated church properties.

"We sang inspiring vibrant Christian songs as we worked," Leslie Peter said.

"What a challenge for me as I was accustomed to living and moving in the flatlands. In the flatlands, I felt comfortable and safe."

This whole Summer was a challenge for me to apply myself. I am prone to procrastinate and be limited by doubts, discouragement and indecision. Aside from developing my mind and freeing it from the limitations of doubt and dread, I learned that life doesn't give you many second changes. God does."

Jean Alerte said, "You have to apply a great deal of hard work and dedication to accomplish any- thing of great value." (p.70.)

"Life has the strangest way of educating us. Every day, we learn something new." (p. 70.)

"According to Proverbs, the lazy person should take a lesson from the ant and learn their ways because ants, having no guide, no over seer or someone to rule over them, still work hard every day to gather their food." (Proverbs 6:6-8.)

Alerte said, "So, if the ants can reach their quota in gathering food for their harvest, why can't you work hard in perfecting your craft so you can live a better life. You become diligent when you learn to work hard." (p.49.)

CHAPTER XIV

Twenty Cups of Coffee a Day

"Almost equal to the Rocky Mountains daily travel challenge was the challenge for me, a non-coffee drinker, to drink a cup of coffee in each home visited, roughly twenty cups a day. Coffee is the Blackfoot Indian's drink of choice. Refusal or failure to drink coffee with a Blackfoot Indian is to reject him and distance yourself from him," stated Leslie Peter.

"Sharing a drink of coffee with him is to accept him, embrace him and engender a good, warm, wholesome and fruitful pastoral visit."

"Three Summer months of working in the heat of Montana, with a strange group of people, the Blackfoot Indians and with whites was sometimes very taxing and tedious.

Leslie Peter told us, "I felt isolated and lonely and sometimes even frightened."

Sometimes my agoraphobia became worse, my whole health system changed.

(Let me explain my phobia.)

"A phobia is an exaggerated or irrational fear of an object, activity or situation that poses no real danger. Phobias provoke overwhelming levels of anxiety and intense reactions that dramatically impact a person's life. Gradually and repeatedly facing such fears have helped many to overcome phobias." (RIVERSIDE WEBSTER'S II NEW COLLEGE DICTIONARY and David Egner, OVERCOMING WORRY, P. 6).

I had all I could do to keep from regurgitating sometimes in front of the Blackfoot Indian that I was visiting. My dislike for coffee, especially their type of coffee and sugar (or non-sugar) heightened. Some nights I felt like weeping. Weeping!

"No! I just felt like crying and I did."

"I felt that this was a place where few, if any persons outside the Blackfoot Indian had been or traveled."

I wondered, "How can these people live like this. How can other human beings allow fellow human beings not feel the pain experienced by such sub-standard living."

I was young and inexperienced and sometimes wanted to go home to my people. Then, I would think, but these are my people.

Reverend James Bell and Leslie Peter, along with other volunteers, helped this group of Indians weather the storm and realize that there is a better life. Their journey through a hard life started a new birth. The Blackfoot Indian had hard life issues but had endured them from generation to generation.

They had developed a positive outlook on life which was staggering to the outside world.

Leslie Peter said, "We were fortunate just to know and witness their simple way of life and to know that God had sustained the Blackfoot Indian over the years with his love and grace.

CHAPTER XV

Leslie Peter's Experiences in Mennonite Biblical Seminary

Leslie Peter served as an exchange student at a Mennonite Biblical Seminary while still at Gammon Theological Seminary. The Mennonite Seminary is based in Elkhart, Indiana. This also was a great experience for Leslie.

Some say that the Mennonite society came out of the Amish community. While Amish people live a very secluded quiet life more like the Quakers of another period, the Mennonites live in a more open modern society.

Leslie Peter's great experiences in Elkhart, Indiana were with a loving group of people. He was well accepted in the seminary and in the community.

Leslie Peter said in his book, GOD'S EARLY MORNING INTERVENTION, "God is omnipotent, preeminent and ultimate leader of the world. Notwithstanding, God is not coercive. God periodically intervenes in our lives and circumstances, and does so without forcing us to obey Him or follow His lead."

"When we follow God's lead, we are following the lead of the ultimate universal leader, the One who knows the way and is the way."

It was an interesting and rewarding sight to see how the Mennonites lived and solved their problems. "The twenty-first century has come upon us like gangbusters. Many of us seem discombobulated and dumbfounded by and unprepared for the multiplicity of challenges in the twenty-first - century. Many of us are still living in the twentieth-century mind set." (para,)

"Yet, there was so much joy in that seminary and society. I served as an intern."

BLESS BE THE TIES THAT BINDS
OUR HEARTS IN CHRISTIAN LOVE;
THE FELLOWSHIP OF KINDRED MINDS
IS LIKE TO THAT ABOVE.

Words: John Fawcett, 1782. (Dennis S.M.)
(Used by Charles Wesley)
THE UNITED METHODIST HYMNAL

CHAPTER XVI

Leslie Peter's Ministrial Career

Leslie Peter has had a glorious time in the ministry. He is leaving his legacy where ever he leaves his foot prints. He has faith which is the greatest benefit of his purpose in life that opened up his mind to the purpose for which he was created. He has learned in great detail just what his qualities entail and how they were acquired, developed and incorporated into his strategy and strengths.

"His biographical sketch reveals that he had great seminary experiences, was ordained elder in 1964 with his best friend, Bertrand Griffin – the only two ministers ordained that day. They were admitted into full connection in the Louisiana Conference.

Leslie Peter served various Louisiana appointments: Hartzell and Mt Zion churches in Slidell, La. And Haven church, Bethany church and Mount Zion church, all in New Orleans in succession.

Leslie Peter became the Louisiana Conference Executive Secretary of Christian Education for several years.

Then he was given the position of Chaplain and Assistant Professor of Religion at Dillard University where he enjoyed teaching theology history courses and preaching to the students on Sunday morning and Wednesday mid-day.

Meanwhile, Leslie Peter served on numerous church, civic and university boards.

He was appointed Baton Rouge District Superintendent until his retirement in 2001.

Although retired, Leslie Peter served as the Louisiana Conference Vision 2000 steering committee and was Chairperson of the Worship Task Force. He was appointed as vice president of the Methodist Children's Home board of directors.

Leslie Peter was a charter member of the ALL CONGREGATIONS TOGETHER (ACT) serving as the first vice president and nominating committee chairperson.

To his credit, Leslie Peter has had a splendid, adventurous and courageous life in the ministry:

1. First exchange student in Interdenominational Theological Center history, 1962,
2. As clergy intern and pastor, he served churches within the geographical boundaries of every jurisdiction in United Methodism,
3. Listed in WHO'S WHO IN THE METHODIST CHURCH, 1966,
4. Outstanding Achievement Award, Dillard University, Student Government Association, 1976,
5. Outstanding Service Award, Alpha Phi Omega National Service Fraternity, 1987
6. New Orleans City Council, 1986.
7. Outstanding Service Award, National Head Start Association, 1987
8. Minister of the Year Award, Civilian Club, 1990
9. Louisiana delegate, WORLD METHODIST CONFERENCE, Singapore, Asia, 1991; Rio de Janeiro, Brazil, 1996; Brighton, England, 2001
10. First of five Louisiana Norris clergy to retire, June 2001 (Three Norris Clergymen died in active service).

(Taken from his book, Leslie P. Norris, Jr. GOD'S EARLY MORNING INTERVENTION).

CHAPTER XVII

Leslie Peter's Non-Humpty Dumpty Experience

"On September 14, 2006, Reporter Robert Stanton wrote in the Houston Chronicle, "Three years ago, the Rev. Leslie Norris suffered a stroke. Last year on August 29, 2005, he and his family lost their home in New Orleans to Hurricane Katrina." It was the same day that Leslie Peter, IV celebrated his birthday. The family was leaving their home forever on their son's birthday. August was a sad but happy day.

"Now, he is keeping a positive outlook as he settles down to a new life in Pearland, Texas. State of the art medical advances are helping him regain some of the mobility his stroke took from him." (p.5).

Leslie Peter's latest experiences were NOT Humpty Dumpty ones. He does not crack under pressure. After a conversation with his three -year old Granddaughter Aria, about the many events and issues in his life, both good and bad, Grandpa Leslie and Grandma Roszeta heard their only granddaughter say, "Grandpa, that's not funny, and I'm not laughing."

The whole adult family members laughed at this child's statement.

The newspaper article states: "STROKE, HURRICANE CAN'T KEEP MAN FROM STAYING OPTIMISTIC! Katrina evacuee recuperating at new home in Pearland, Texas!"

"First he suffered a paralyzing stroke. Then Hurricane Katrina uprooted his family from New Orleans. Despite it all, the Rev. Leslie Norris never lost faith that his life would return to normal."

"He couldn't have been more right!"

Leslie Peter, 66 years old (in 2006), told the reporter, "Some people talk faith, and I have met many folks who throw in the towel whenever they get a real, supreme challenge. I never lost my faith in God, and that is what has brought me through this and causes me to be confident from day to day."

"I can do all things through Christ which strengthens me."

"Cling to what is good. Be devoted to one another in brotherly love. Honor one another above yourselves Never be lacking in zeal, but keep your spiritual fervor, serving the Lord." (Romans 12: 9-11, NIV).

"Be joyful in hope, patient in affliction, faithful in prayer." (Romans 12: 12).

PART THREE

CHAPTER XVIII

Eleanor Seals Miles

Eleanor S is my very best friend. She is one hundred and two years old. She was born in Clinton, Louisiana to Amelia Davis and Charlie Seals on February 26, 1917, the last daughter born to this union. She is the only sibling still alive.

She is the youngest child of eleven children. She was a twin and that twin sister, Elnora, died in child-birth She had five sisters whom she adored. Her other four sisters were Beatrice Davis, Margaret Davidson, Leona Pearson, Bessie William.

Her five brothers were Rayfield, Columbia "Chris", Johnnie, Isaac and Lee.

Eleanor S said, "I have had a glorious life. I was born in the country. My family protected me all my days and took good care of me. I learned to trust in God at a very early age."

"I had a wonderful husband for over forty years. He was an old country style preacher. James had three teen age children when I met him.

Oftentimes, I had to pray about them because they resented me. I tried my best to treat them as best that I could. I was dealing with the only crisis or difficulty in my life at the time, but I didn't want my husband to know how deeply hurt I was when his children ignored and disregarded me. He loved his children dearly and I loved him dearly.

Joanna Lauper states in her book, INSPIRED: THE BREATH OF GOD, "When we go through hardships and trials- though we often credit our healing to emotional support, resilience and time, many of us sense a mysterious stirring within us. This is a stirring that tells us that something larger than us is at work, that something is filling our spirits and inspiring us to press on." (p. 6).

"We may never be able to understand a gun pointed at an infant's head, the loss and cruel experiences during the Holocaust, but we may be able to understand, in hindsight, or as it happens – that God is present in our blessings and in our trials.

We read in the book of Job that "there is a spirit in man and the inspiration of the Almighty giveth them understanding," (Job 32: 18, KJV).

"To know this is to know our limits as human beings."

"We do not have God's understanding on our own. We do not have his vision. When we become inspired, we are granted a moment of hearing or seeing what we ordinarily do not hear or see. We are filled with an elevated understanding and vision that lifts us up above our grief and hurt and elevates the quality of our work." (INSPIRED, p. 6-7).

Margaret Peterson wrote in CIRCLES OF LOVE:

THE HARMONY OF LIFE

How can man live without God, Who gave him his very life. He, the one we turn to in prayer, and calms us in times of strife.

Eleanor was constantly praying:

"You are my rock and my Fortress; for your name sake, lead and guide me." (Psalms 31: 4, NIV).

CHAPTER XIX

Eleanor's Move to Baton Rouge

"When I moved to Baton Rouge, Louisiana, I joined St. Mark United Methodist Church and have been a member for over eighty- five years and attended church every Sunday until my health started failing me," Eleanor told me.

"I have served St. Mark United Methodist Church for over eighty years, and sang in the Chancel Choir for many many years.

I attended the elements of Christ as a communion steward for over forty years. I am a faithful member of the United Methodist Women, L.B. Lewis Study Group and enjoy every meeting, under the guidance of Edna Hickman. I have held many offices in my church and love all the members.

"I served as Eastern Star District Deputy for thirty years. I traveled many miles with this group of ladies. We had so many good times together. I met so many good and faithful people over the years."

Eleanor said, "But most of all, I enjoyed my job as a nurse and a sitter. It was such a blessing to me and I tried to make it a blessing to all those that I served."

"I looked at all my patients as persons made in the image of God. We were all made in the image of God."

"I had been trained well to do my job. I had learned to provide the best of care to my patients. I encouraged them and supported them. I provided a variety of ways to aid them in their life changing situations as they had varying degrees of disabilities in their lives," she said.

Eleanor said, "I was industrious; I designed ways to help my patients master and relearn skills and basic functions that were needed to thrive as they aged. I tried to develop ways to help them have fun and relax with others."

Lauper said, "When the divine Spirit enlivens us, there is the hope that, in turn, this will stir the spirits of others. We aim to show how the spirit of God has inspired us in our work, love and trials." (Para. p.6).

CHAPTER XX

Beatrice Became Ill

Eleanor said many times, "My oldest sister, Beatrice, became ill. She had helped to take care of our parents until they passed. Now it was her turn to need someone important in her life to care for her.

"I terminated all of my other sitter jobs and became my sister's 'around the clock' caregiver."

"We had many things in common, a caring nature, a good sense of humor, a love of people in need."

"It felt strange to be caring for someone who had cared for me all my life. Yet, it felt so right."

"Her comfort and needs were all I cared about as I tried to nurse her back to health. Sometimes she would cry at night. I cried with her."

"The horrors of her pain that I witnessed, carved scares that ran deep into my soul. Yet, she prayed. I prayed in hopes that she would find relief from her suffering. Every waking moment weighed heavy on my heart."

"To pray is to listen, also. I just wanted to do what God wanted me to do."

"In our prayers, we accept that "this is not just a monologue, that God not only listens, but He responds, not with a big booming voice, but to the heart- the way the heart speaks to us about love."

Sometimes I wondered what to do to help! We didn't have all the answers, but God did. I realized that it's OK to not have all the answers. We don't know how God is going to do it. Not even did Paul know how God was going to solve his many problems and he wrote half of the New Testament.

God said, "Lean not on your own understanding." (Proverbs 3: 5-6. KJV).

"When we make ourselves available and hear or feel God's response, it is subtle but unmistakable, like the act of breathing."

Job in chapter 33: 4, said, "The spirit of God has made me, the breath of the Almighty gives me life." (NIV).

"Bea survived many days crammed with pain and agony. She endured all the therapies and other life-changing support services that were given to her."

"One after the other, my four older sisters became ill. First, Beatrice was sick and bed ridden. Then Margaret and Leona and Bessie in succession became ill. As I attempted to care for each sister, I felt so overwhelmed, inadequate and useless. My sisters seemed so helpless on their sick beds."

We develop unrealistic expectations of ourselves and our Christian lives that when we falter, we think that we have failed and we are useless.

Some of David's greatest psalms came after he made big mistakes. Yet, God called him a "man after his own heart." (I Samuel 13: 14, NIV).

Many of us know too well the bad feeling of failure. It helps us to remember that even great men (women) of faith sometimes fail. Yet, God continues to use them, often in a deeper way after their failure.

"God calls us to shepherd others, to care for them even after we plunge into the depth of failure and helplessness," Eleanor stated.

"I often felt so helpless while I was sitting with one of my sisters and watched her in agony. I realized that I was trained to do this work. We had to wait on the medicine to work. We had to wait on God. Through our emotional and physical pain, we look for God to show up every day. It is worth the wait.

"Trust in the Lord with all thine heart and lean not unto thine own understanding. In all thy ways acknowledge Him and He will direct thy path." (Proverbs 3: 5-6, KJV).

"Prayer became my bulwalk. My life seemed filled with worries and anxieties. After praying, I could take my eyes off myself and think about the task ahead. I received comfort and encouragement and could give the same to my sisters. God is a God of action. He will help us solve our problems."

Eleanor said, "I was struggling with my own family and had to leave my home to attend to other family members for many years."

Trillia J. Newbell in her book UNITED CAPTURED BY GOD'S VISION FOR DIVERSITY, stated, "While it may have looked like I was discontent, I wasn't. I wasn't grumbling about unmet desires and needs for myself." (Para. p. 59).

"I longed for more understanding as I tried to navigate my own feeling. I wanted my sisters and family to have peace and grace."

"I got tired sometimes, but every time I wanted to give up and quit, I was visited by an angel. With the illnesses they had, only God could bring about life-changing events in my sister's lives."

"My sister's doctors constantly gave me updates on their prognosis and diagnosis. I couldn't fathom all that they were telling me. All I knew was that they required my full attention."

Napoleon Hills spelled out in his book, KEYS TO SUCCESS, that a "purpose in life develops self-reliance, personal initiative, imagination, enthusiasm, self-descriptive and concentrated effort." (para. p. 3).

All of these qualities are required for success on whatever task you set out to do and "makes you aware of the opportunities to bring a host of other advantages including integrity and character, which attracts favorable attention from others and inspires their cooperation." (Para. p. 4).

CHAPTER XXI

Eleanor On My Mind

FAST FORWARD:

"Last night, I thought was my last. What is wrong, I thought. I couldn't eat even though I was hungry. I could not breathe, no matter how hard I tried. I could not sleep."

"Last night I silently begged my Creator for mercy."

"Today I am receiving His mercy. He never breaks a promise. God also said "Whatever you ask in my name, believe in me, and I will do it."

I sat with my one hundred two (102) year old 'proxy mother' yesterday. She had called me.

"Can you come over," she said.

"I am hurting really bad and I have something to tell you and I don't want anyone else to hear me"

I got my husband, Bertrand up out of bed. I said "something is wrong with Eleanor. She just called and said she had something to tell me and she didn't want anyone else to hear her."

When we got to my buddy's house, my husband kissed her on the forehead and said "God bless you."

"I sat down next to her. These were our usual ways of greeting Eleanor."

She thanked my husband for that kiss and said she needed it because she was hurting so bad.

I started quizzing her as to whether she had taken her medicine and had the home health nurse come the day before?

She said 'yes' to all my questions.

"Remember, you were supposed to have Miss T take you to your primary doctor two days ago and you wouldn't go. You said you were hurting too bad to go see him."

"I was reading the signs of my special friend, Eleanor feeling isolated, lonely and perhaps a little depressed."

She said, "I've never felt like this before. I feel like I am losing myself, losing control of myself."

"I've always been able to take care of myself, always self-sufficient since I as a little girl. I could fight for myself and for my older sisters."

"I'd plow into someone if they were fussing with one of my sisters."

"Who taught you how to fight?" I asked, trying to keep the conversation going.

"My brothers taught me how to fight, so that if one of them was not with me, I could fight for myself."

My retort was, "My brothers taught me how to take care of myself, too. The best fighter is one whose brother taught her how to defend herself."

"I said, "You always say you have never been one hundred and two years old before, either. Well you are one hundred and two and five months now. You are beginning to smell your own piss."

Eleanor cracked up laughing and said, "You're a mess. I don't know how I put up with you."

"We were both laughing. That was the response that I wanted."

My husband, Bertrand told her, "God is not through with you, yet. You can't go anywhere until he is ready for you. You have a little more work to do down here. So, settle down, don't panic. God will call you when he is ready for you."

"Then she started telling me all the persons who had not called her lately."

She said, "Vera and Sonora haven't called. Eloise used to call me every day.

"Oh, I remember, they all died a long time ago. If I could just get out of this wheel chair, I could go see my friends."

"Eleanor," I will have to suffice for Vera and Sonora and Eloise, because they have gone on to Glory. We're still here with you and you just have to let us do for the time being."

We both had a good laugh. Her day had been stressful and painful. My day had been frustrating and sad.

"Was Eleanor slipping away from us. I tried to cheer her up."

It is no wonder the Scripture says, "A cheerful heart is good medicine, but a broken spirit saps a person's strength." (Proverbs 17: 22, NIV.)

Jeanette Hanscome said in MORNINGS WITH JESUS that "I feel closer to Jesus when I laugh and see the humor in circumstances. Seeing His sense of fun reflected in His creation, reminds me that He is the ultimate source of joy and that we serve a Lord who understands that, with all that life throws at us, sometimes the best thing we can do is laugh. (p. 14.)

"All joking aside, Marian. I have never hurt like this before. I want you to find me another doctor," Eleanor told me.

I said, "You didn't keep your appointment on Wednesday, two days ago. You told me you didn't feel like seeing him. Now you tell me you want a new doctor; you don't like this one anymore?"

"What happened?"

"He's not doing anything for me, he just asks me a few questions, and types on his computer."

"His nurse will call me and say, "Eleanor, it's time for you to come see your doctor. I'm setting up your appointment for Tuesday, no Wednesday.""

"Don't call me Eleanor, I'm old enough to be your great-Grandmother," I want to tell her.

"Eleanor, I call you by your first name. I have called you Eleanor, every since I've known you."

"Yah, but, you're "First Lady. You're my 'First Lady' and I respect you as a minister's wife."

"We respect each other, both as minister's wives."

"Anyway, I called the appointment desk of Eleanor's doctor. The doctor was on a clinical mission with other doctors. The desk let me talk to a nurse who was a supervising nurse."

"I put the phone on speaker and we talked to the nurse together."

"Eleanor told the nurse, "I'm not going to the emergency room, I don't feel like going."

Eleanor told me "Hang up on her. She talks too much." Eleanor was getting loud.

The nurse was trying to get Eleanor's demographic so she could report that Eleanor had refused service.

"I told the nurse that I would have to call her back."

"Eleanor was becoming very irate and hateful."

"Calm down, Eleanor. Where is your medicine?" I asked.

"Right here in my purse. It's not time for me to take it right now."

"Well, I'm going to find you a pain pill. You said your leg was hurting really bad, and you need some relief. There is no need for you to be suffering like this."

"From my own experience of working with persons, I was not a nurse or doctor, but I was a Psychological Counselor."

I had observed other people in severely painful situations like this. They tend to feel as if they were running out of resources. One of the characteristics is a need to control- they need to control their life, their circumstances, the people around them and ultimately God. It was not just a physical circumstance; it was their total being.

Eleanor seemed afraid of what might happen to herself. She had built a wall, a cocoon around herself. She was panicky. She wanted no one inside her cocoon but me. She seemed to feel only a small space in which she felt secure and safe.

"I began to feel nervous but couldn't show it."

"Eleanor was having problems I had not seen before. She had developed a bitterness toward her doctor; she wanted to be self-sufficient and self-reliant, yet she was showing an immaturity and an inability to handle herself and responsibility for her own health."

"She never wants anyone to spend the night in her house. She's afraid she will wake up and hear someone in her house and shoot them. She sleeps with her German Luger pistol near her hand."

"I was preparing to spend the night with her in another bed room."

"Eleanor had dozed off for her usual three o'clock nap. However, she overheard me telling my husband to go home and get some rest."

"She woke up and said, No, both of you go home and get some rest. I can take care of myself. I feel much better now. Go on home, I'm OK. I'll call you tomorrow."

"There was nothing I could do but abide by her wishes. When I got home, I called one of her young neighbors who checks on her every day when he gets home from work. He was not home. (He told me later, that he had gone to New Orleans for the week-end.)

"I prayed all night. I couldn't sleep that night; I couldn't eat. I had taken on Eleanor's pain and suffering. Bertrand gave me some pain medicine, I regurgitated it up. He tried to get me to eat, I couldn't stomach any food.

I had done what I was taught not to do in my psych classes. Do not transfer your feelings onto someone else and do not accept transferal of their feelings on yourself. I had done just that. I laid awake all night worrying about the fate of my friend, Eleanor. I had a recognized fear that something tragic, yet wonderful, would happen.

Before I left her side, I saw a tear on Eleanor's eye lid. I had never seen Eleanor cry before. But through her many experiences in life, she has cried different kinds of tears.

We may realize that shedding a tear at certain times will have a particular effect upon us. What we are probably less conscious of is that each tear regardless of its origin or its effect contains a seed of healing. As I left, "I told Eleanor to pray and wait on the Lord. I will, too."

CONCLUSION

Life has the strangest way of educating us. Our background often determines who we are or what we will be.

Years ago, when I was a child, I thought like a child, I acted like a child. I spoke like a child. Now I am grown, I think like a child. I act out of pure love; I know no other way.

"A little child shall lead them." I have worked with children with music and art since I was a child, twelve years old going into junior high or middle school," I told my grandchildren.

"I wasn't even old enough to discipline the children I was working with. I had to ask my own elementary school teacher, Miss Daniels, to help me work with the small children because I was only a child myself. All I could do was play the music on the piano and teach them how to sing it."

"I didn't know this was a part of these children's evolving or developing into their purpose in life."

When I look into the face of a child, I may be looking a Newton, Voltaire, Langton Hughes or Maya Angelou or Barack Obama, all of who had difficult childhoods in some form or another.

Dennis Kimbro, said in his Forward to Alente's book, DO RIGHT, DO GOOD, "Nothing is coincidental. I am convinced that many times in the course of our lives, the Creator challenges us to be more and do more than what we think is possible. No one suggests that you accept that challenge by listening to the still voice within you. and taking the first step." (p. vii.)

So many of us, like newly born turtles, are at risk at birth. We should all have a chance in life. God made each of us as a unique individual. We each have a purpose to fulfill. How we react or fail to react to our God given purpose in life will determine the course of our future.

An individual told Alerte, "I think you should write a book."

Alerte's reply was" Why, what would I write about.?"

His friend replied, "About yourself and your life."

"I am writing a story about three people that I know fairly well, yet, I don't know them that well. There are so many questions in my mind about each of them that is blank to me. That is because they are still growing, still maturing, still emerging, still in the process of evolving into a creation that God made. Each day is a new high for them," I say.

Every day of your life, God is working in you and through you. You will have set-backs and curve-balls thrown at you.

Mark and Angel Chernoff, In their book, GETTING BACK TO HAPPY, announced, "Our journeys have been anything but easy and we have been forced to re-invent ourselves personally and professionally. We should be wholeheartedly grateful for the lessons we glean as we walk our way through it one day at a time." (Para. p. xv.)

We may realize or discover that we don't really have control over our lives.

"In the game of life, we each receive a unique set of unexpected limitations and variable questions. How will you respond to the hand you've been dealt? You can either face what you are lacking or empower yourself to play the game sensibly or resourcefully." (Chernoff, para, p. 219,)

It's important to "communicate with the people who matter to you-people who add value to your life is essential to you. Use your voice for good, to inspire, encourage, to educate and spread the type of behavior you want to see in others." (para. p. 212.)

Bertrand Griffin, my ministerial husband tells people, "Every day that you live, is a new day. God is not through with you yet. Keep breathing, keep living. You will be rewarded."

Where is my voice. I want to hear my voice. No one gets through life without disruptions and obstructions. It is these trials and tribulations that make us strong and eventually moves us toward future opportunities. New opportunities are there waiting for us.

Each day moves us to a new high! AT THE END OF THE DAY, YOU ARE YOUR GREATEST ASSET.

BIBLIOGRAPHY

Adam, Elaine Parker, THE REVEREND PETER W. CLARK. Indiana: Wesbow Press Books, 2013.

Alerte, Jean. DO RIGHT, DO GOOD. New York: Zangbe Thomson, 2012.

Anderson, Joan Wester, GAURDIAN ANGELS. Illinois: Loyola Press, 2006.

Angelou, Maya. I KNOW WHY THE CAGED BIRD SINGS. New York: Random House, 1989.

--------------------. LETTERS TO MY DAUGHTER. New York: Random House. 2008.

--------------------RAINBOW IN THE CLOUDS. New York: Random House, 2014.

--------------------THE HEART OF A WOMAN. New York: Random House, 1982

Armour, Vernice. ZERO TO BREAKTHROUGH. New York: Gotham Publishing Co., 2011.

Barboza, Steven, ed. THE AFRICAN AMERICAN BOOK OF VALUES. New York: Doubleday Publishing Co. 1998.

Bernard, Emily, BLACK IS THE BODY. New York: Penguin Random House, LLC., 2000.

Billingley, Reshonda Tate. THE MOTHERHOOD DIARIES. New York: Stebor, 2013.

Blake, Barry. THE BLESSING OF ADVERSITY. Illinois: Tyndale House Publishing Co.,

Blake, Charles E. FREE TO DREAM. California: Albany Publishing co., 2000.

Blanco, Richard. FOR ALL OF US, ONE TODAY New York: Beacon Press, 2013.

Bloomer, George. THROW OFF WHAT HOLDS YOU BACK. Florida: Charisma House, A Strange Co, 2003.

Bodanis, David. PASSIONATE MINDS. New York: Crown Publishing Group, 2006.

Boers. Arthur Paul. THE WAY IS MADE BY WALKING. Illinois: Inter Varsity Press, 2007.

Booker, Dianna. SPEAK WITH CONFIDENCE. New York: McGraw, 2003.

Brandon, Dave. TOGETHER WITH GOD; PSALMS. Michigan: Discovery. 2016.

Brown, James. ROLE OF ALIFE TIME. New York: Hachatte Book Group, 2009.

Buttworth, Eria. THE CREATIVE LIFE. New York: Penguin, Inc. 2001.

Coates, Ta-Nehisi. BETWEEN THE WORLD AND ME. New York: Spiegal and Grua, 2015.

Chernoff, Marc & Angel. GETTING BACK TO HAPPY. New York: Penguin Random, 2018.

Cormer, James P. and Alvin Poussaint. RAISING BLACK CHILDREN. New York: Penguin, 1992.

Cose, Ellis. THE END OF ANGER. New York: HarperCollins Publishing Co. 2011.

Cunningham, Loren & David Joel Hamilton. WHY NOT WOMEN. Washington: Youth with A Mission, 2000.

Delinsky, Barbara. FAMILY TREE. New York Doubleday Co. 2007.

Fredman, Edwin H. GENERATION TO GENERATION. New York: The Guilford Press, 1985.

Habegger, Alfred. MY WARS ARE LAID AWAY IN BOOKS. New York: The Modern Library, 2001.

Hart, Kevan. I CAN'T MAKE THIS UP.

Harris, Kamala. THE TRUTHS WE HOLD. New York: Penguin Press, 2019.

Hibbert, Christina. WHO AM I WITHOUT YOU? Calif: New Harbinger Publishers, 2015.

Hill, Napoleon. KEYS TO SUCCESS. New York: Penguin Group, 1997.

Hoffman, Hazel & Audrey McDomic. THE GREATEST OF THESE IS LOVE. Conn: The C. R. Gibson Co, 1962.

Howard, Thomas, ed. BLACK VOYAGE. Boston: Little, Brown and Co. 1971.

Hunter, Kristin. GOD BLESS THE CHILD. New York: Scribner Publishing Co, 1964.

Hyatt, Michael. YOUR BEST YEAR EVER. Michigan: Baker Books, 2018.

Jackson, John G. INTRODUCTION OF AFRICAN CIVILIZATION. Canada: Carol Publishing Co. 1970.

Kate, Frederick Ward. BENEATH DAWN AND DARK. The Upper Room Nashville: 1957.

Kerr, Miranda. TREASURE YOURSELF. New York Hay House, Inc. 2012.

Kimbro, Dennis P. WHAT MAKES THE GREAT GREAT? New York: Penguin Group, 1997.

Lee, June N. THE BLACK FAMILY. Michigan: Zondervan Publishing House, 1991.

Laufer, Joanna, & Kenneth S. Lewis, INSPIRED: THE BREATH OF GOD. New York: Doubleday, 1998.

Leon, Kenny TAKE YOU WHEREVER YOU GO. New York: Grand Central Publishing Co., 2018.

Lieberson, S. A. A PIECE OF THE PIE. Calif: University of California Press, 1980.

Linn, Matthew and Linn, Dennis. HEALING THE EIGHT STAGES OF LIFE. New York: Paul's Press. 1988.

Malcolm X. BY ANY MEANS NECESSARY. New York: Pathfinder Press, 1970.

Mbugua, Judy. OUR TIME HAS COME. London: The Guerney Press Co, 1994.

Moore, Darnell J. NO ASHES IN THE FIRE. New York: Nation Books, 2018.

Myers, Ruth. 31 DAYS OF PRAISE. New York: Crown Publishing Group, 1994.

Newbell, Trillia J. UNTED CAPTURED BY GOD'S VISION FOR DIVERSITY. Chicago: Moody Press, 2014.

Norris, P. Leslie, Jr. GOD'S EARLY MORNING INTERVENTION. Indiana: Xlibris, 2016.

Nouwen, Henri. REACHING OUT. New York: Doubleday Co. 1975.

Obama, Barack. DREAMS OF MY FATHER. New York: Crown Publishing Group, 2004.

-------------------- THE AUDACITY OF HOPE. New York: Crown Publishing Group, 1996.

Oliver, Stephanie Stokes. SEVEN SOULFUL SECRETS. New York: Doubleday, 2001.

Pasteur, Alfred and Ivory Toldson. ROOTS OF SOUL. New York: Doubleday Press, 1982.

Peck, M. Scott. FURTHER ALONG THE ROAD LESS TRAVELED. New York: Simon & Schuster Co. 1994.

Rainey, Cortez R. FREE YOUR MIND. Create/Space Independent Publishing Platform 2015.

Rabey, Lois Mowday. WOMEN OF A GENEROUS SPIRIT. Colorado: Waterbrook Press, 1998.

Rath Tom & Donald O. Clifton, Ph.D. HOW FULL IS YOUR BUCKET? New York: Gallup Press, 2004.

Reynolds, Edward. STAND THE STORM. Chicago: Ivan R. Dee, Inc. 1985.

Richardson Cheryl. TAKE TIME FOR YOUR LIFE. New York: Broadway Books, 1998.

Roberson GilL. FAMILY AFFAIR. Canada: agate Publishing, Inc. 2009.

Rosanoff, Nancy. PH. D. KNOWING WHEN IT'S RIGHT. Illinois: Sourcebooks, Inc. 2002.

Russell, A.L. ed. GOD CALLING Ohio: Barbour Publishing Co. 1993

Sanders, Delasber Griffin. NO GREATER LOVE PARENTING THROUGH MULTIPLE DIAGNOSES. Louisiana, 2919.

Selye, H. THE STRESS OF LIFE. New York: MeGraw-Hill Publishing Co. 1956.

Steel, Danielle. AGAINST ALL ODDS. New York: Random House. 2017.

--------------------. PRECIOUS GIFTS. New York: Random House, 2015.

Smiley, Tavis. FAIL UP.

Smarsh, Sarah. HEARTLAND. New York: Simon & Schuster, Inc. 2018.

Smart, Elizabeth. MY STORY. New York: St. Martin Press, 2013.

Storr, Anthony. SOLITUDE: A RETURN TO SELF. New York: Free Press, 1988.

Storoni, Mithu. STRESS PROOF. New York: Castle Point Publishing, LLC, 2018.

Swensom, Kristin M. LIVING THROUGH PAIN. Texas: Baylor University, 2005.

Strahan, Michael. WAKE UP HAPPY. New York: Atria, 2015.

Thernstrom, Abigail and Stephan Thernstrom. NO EXCUSES CLOSING THE RACIAL GAP IN LEARNING. New York: Simon Schuster Publishing Co., 2003.

Tominey, Shanna CREATING COMPASSIONATE KIDS. New York: W.W. Norton & Co. 2019.

Trott, James H. A SACRIFICE OF PRAISE. Nashville: Cumberland House Publishing, 1999.

Walker, Alice. POSSESSING THE SECRET OF JOY. Boston: Compass press, 1993.

Walsh, Dan & Gary Smalley. THE PROMISE. New York: Thorndike Press, 2014.

Watkins, Tionne. A SICK LIFE. New York: Rodale Books, 2017.

Wilder, Howard B., ed. THIS IS AMERICA'S STORY. Boston: Houghton Mifflin Co. 1970.

Williams, Juan. MY SOUL LOOKS BACK AND WONDERS.

Williams, Ted. A GOLDEN VOICE. New York: Penguin Group, 2012.

Williams, Terrie. A PLENTIFUL HARVEST. New York: Warner Books Inc., 2002.

Winch, Guy, Ph.D. EMOTIONAL FIRST AID. New York: Hudson Street Press, 2013.

Winfrey, Oprah. WHAT I KNOW FOR SURE.

Zook, Kristal. BLACK WOMEN'S LIVES. New York: Nations Books, 2017.

REFERENCE BOOKS

AFRICAN AMERICAN HERITAGE HYMNAL. Chicago: GIA Publications, Inc., 2001.

Laird, Charlton. WEBSTER'S NEW ROGER'S A-Z THESAURUS. Cleveland, Ohio: Wilet Publishing Co, 2003.

Riverside's II New College Dictionary. New York: Houghton Miffin Co., 1995

THE HOLY BIBLE. New International Version. Michigan: Vondervan, 1973.

THE NEW ENCYCLOPEDIA BRITANNICA, Volume 1-26. Chicago: ENCYCLOPEDIA BRITANNICA Inc. 1768-1771, Fifteenth edition, 1986.

THE UNITED METHODIST HYMNAL. Book of United Methodist Worship, Nashville: The United Methodist Publishing House, 1989.

Printed in the United States
By Bookmasters